LANCASH

Teashop Walks

Jean Patefield

COUNTRYSIDE BOOKS
NEWBURY BERKSHIRE

First published 2000
© Jean Patefield 2000

COUNTRYSIDE BOOKS
3 Catherine Road
Newbury, Berkshire

To view our complete range of books,
please visit us at
www.countrysidebooks.co.uk

ISBN 1 85306 607 9

Designed by Graham Whiteman
Cover illustration by Colin Doggett
Maps and photographs by the author

Produced through MRM Associates Ltd., Reading
Typeset by Techniset Typesetters, Newton-le-Willows
Printed by J. W. Arrowsmith Ltd., Bristol

Contents

Walk

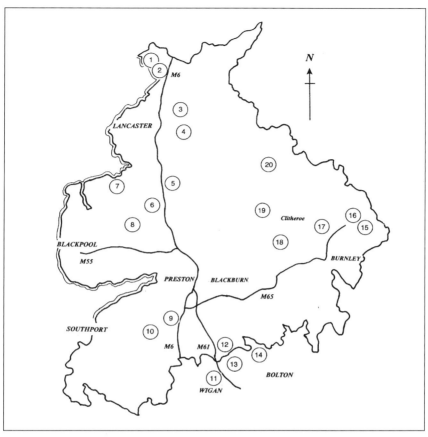

Area map showing the locations of the walks.

KEY TO SKETCH MAPS

Path on route	$--\rightarrow$	Sea, lake or pond	~ ~ ~	Point in text	⑤
Path not on route	...	Church	†	Car park	☐
Road	═══	Teashop	☕	Building or feature referred to in text	■
River, stream or canal	∿∿∿	Pub referred to in text	PH	Railway	⊢⊢⊢)(⊢⊢

Introduction

Let me confess plainly at the outset that I approached the preparation of this book consumed by the deepest prejudice. I am a Lancashire lass by birth and upbringing and I was delighted to have the opportunity to share the delights of my native county and introduce its lovely countryside to a wider audience.

My introduction to walking was by youthful expeditions to the Bleasdale Fells. The excitement of catching a red Ribble bus from Blackpool bus station to Garstang and setting off to wander all day in the hills has never left me and started me on a lifetime's pleasure.

Lancashire was the dynamic heartland of the Industrial Revolution. Many do not see beyond the legacy of that contribution as they hurtle through on the M6 to the Mecca of the Lakes or Scotland, perhaps just registering a landscape of rounded fells or the wide sweep of Morecambe Bay. The Red Rose County has much to offer the visitor and those who live with its charms on their doorstep are fortunate indeed. The diversity of the landscape offers an enormous variety of walks to be enjoyed from challenging ascents to breathtaking viewpoints (see Walk 4 up Clougha Pike) to gentle potters exploring charming villages and the attractive countryside between (see Walk 20 round Newton and Slaidburn). There is something to suit every mood and occasion.

There is no National Park in Lancashire but it does have two Areas of Outstanding Natural Beauty – the Forest of Bowland and the Arnside-Silverdale area straddling the border with Cumbria. The Forest of Bowland includes the largest expanse of continuous heather moor in England and is of considerable wildlife significance. The Silverdale area in the far north of the county is a gem and I make no apologies for including two walks in close proximity (Walks 1 and 2). With more space I could have included a dozen, all different and all delightful. Morecambe Bay (see Walk 7) is of international importance for its populations of birds, as is Leighton Moss close by (Walk 2).

There is much of historical interest to explore. Lancashire was, and still is, the most staunchly Catholic county. Not entirely unconnected with that fact is that it is also the most haunted with more spooks per square mile than any other region. Black, white and grey ladies float about long after serving as cover for illegal priestly activity during the time of religious strife (see Walk 14 to Turton Tower). Shocking scandals are remembered to this day (see Walk 17 in the countryside inhabited by the Lancashire witches).

The 20 walks in this book explore the varied landscapes of Lancashire.

They are all between 3 and 7 miles long and should be well within the capacity of the average person, including those of mature years and families with children. They are intended to take the walker through this attractive corner of England at a gentle pace with plenty of time to stop and stare, to savour the beauty and interest all around. A dedicated yomper and stomper could probably knock off the whole book in a single weekend but in doing so they would have missed the point and seen nothing. To fully appreciate the countryside it is necessary to go slowly with your eyes and ears open.

Some of the walks are short and level, ideal for a pipe opener on a winter's day, or giving plenty of time to dawdle away a summer's afternoon. Others are longer or more strenuous, some making an excellent all-day expedition. Certain of the walks involve some climbing. This is inevitable as hills add enormous interest to the countryside and with no hills there are no views. However, this presents no problem to the sensible walker who has three uphill gears – slowly, very slowly and admiring the view. None of the walks in this book are inherently hazardous but sensible care should be taken. Many of the falls that do happen are due to unsuitable footwear, particularly unridged soles since grass slopes can be as slippery as the more obviously hazardous wet, smooth rock. Proper walking shoes or boots also give some protection to the ankle. It is also essential to look where you are putting your feet to avoid tripping up. Wainwright, the doyen of walkers in the Lake District, said that he never had a serious fall in all his years and thousands of miles of walking because he always looked where he put his feet and stopped if he wanted to admire the scenery.

All the routes are on public rights of way or permissive paths and have been carefully checked but, of course, in the countryside things do change; a stile replaces a gate or a wood is extended. Each walk is circular and is illustrated by a sketch map. An Ordnance Survey map is useful as well, especially for identifying the main features of views. The area is covered by the Landranger 1:50 000 (1¼ inches to 1 mile) series, sheets 97, 102, 103, 108 and 109. Even better for walking are the 1:25 000 Explorer 19 and Outdoor Leisure maps 21 and 41. The grid reference of the starting point and the numbers of the appropriate maps are given for each walk.

The walks are designed so that, starting where suggested, the teashop is reached in the second half so a really good appetite for tea can be worked up and then its effects walked off. Some walks start at a car park, which is ideal. Where this is not possible, the suggested starting place will always have somewhere where a few cars can be left without endangering other traffic or causing inconvenience. However, it sometimes fits in better with the plans for the day to start and finish at the teashop and so for each walk there are details of how to do this.

Tea is often said to be the best meal to eat out in England and I believe that it is something to be enjoyed on all possible occasions. Scones with clotted cream and strawberry jam, delicious home-made cakes, toasted teacakes dripping with butter in winter, delicate cucumber sandwiches in summer, all washed down with the cup that cheers. Bad for the figure maybe, but the walking will see to that.

The best teashops serve a range of cakes, all home made and including fruit cake as well as scones and other temptations. Teapots should be capacious and pour properly. Most of the teashops visited on these walks fulfil all these criteria admirably and they all offer a good tea. They always have at least light lunches available as well so there is no need to think of these walks as just something for the afternoons.

There is an abundance of excellent establishments but even so, teashops are not scattered evenly throughout the county. In some places popular with tourists, the visitor is spoilt for choice. In such cases the most convenient teashop that, in the author's opinion, most closely fulfils the criteria set out above is recommended but should that not appeal, there are others from which to choose. In other places where there is a delightful walk to be enjoyed, the choice for tea may be more limited. However, they all offer a good tea partway round an attractive walk. The opening times and telephone number of each teashop are given. Some are rather vague about when they open out of season: it seems to depend on weather and mood. If you are planning a walk on a wet November Tuesday, for example, a call to check that tea will actually be available that day is a wise precaution. A few are definitely closed in the depths of winter and for these walks an alternative source of refreshment is given. In most cases, these are pubs serving food, which in some instances includes tea.

The pleasures of summer walking are obvious. Many of the teashops featured in this book have an attractive garden where tea can be taken outside when the weather is suitable. However, let me urge you not to overlook the pleasures of a good walk in winter. The roads and paths are quieter and what could be better than sitting by an open fire in a cosy teashop scoffing crumpets that you can enjoy with a clear conscience due to the brisk walk to get them!

So put on your walking shoes and prepare to be delighted by the charms of Lancashire and refreshed by a traditional English tea!

Jean Patefield

Walk 1
SILVERDALE

'I think one is never disappointed in coming back to Silverdale', said Victorian novelist Elizabeth Gaskell, writing in 1858. This charming walk illustrates why. It is full of natural and historic interest and I cannot recommend it too highly. Essentially, the route circumnavigates the scattered community of Silverdale but in a few miles it includes lots of attractive woodland, meadows of great botanical importance and splendid views across the Kent estuary and Morecambe Bay. It also gives a fascinating insight into the problems faced by a village built on limestone before modern water supplies were organised.

☕ Wolf House Gallery takes its name from the coat of arms above the door of the adjoining Georgian house. The motto reads 'Homo Homini Lupus' – Man is a Wolf to Man. No such aggression prevails today where old farm buildings have been converted into galleries displaying an attractive range of traditional and contemporary crafts and paintings. The main gallery was once a shippon and now has a cosy tea area at one end. The wood burning stove is especially welcome in winter and much loved by the somnolent cats in residence. The menu is limited to scones and home-made biscuits, such as flapjacks and shortbread, and they are delicious. The Wolf House Gallery is open from 10.30 am to 1 pm and 2 pm to 5.30 pm every day except Monday from Easter until Christmas. From January to Easter they open from 10.30 am through to 5.30 pm on Saturday and Sunday only. Telephone: 01524 701405.

When the teashop is closed there are pubs in Silverdale that serve food.

DISTANCE: 4 miles.

MAP: OS Landranger 97 Kendal and Morecambe.

STARTING POINT: Eaves Wood car park (GR 471759).

HOW TO GET THERE: From the traffic lights on the A6 in the centre of Carnforth take a road, signed 'Silverdale', past the station. On the outskirts of Warton turn left, signed 'Silverdale 3¾'. Continue on the main road, over a level crossing and after a further ¼ mile turn right at a T junction. Pass Silverdale Station and take the next left, Park Road, to Eaves Wood car park after 100 yards on the right.

ALTERNATIVE STARTING POINT:: There is no parking in the vicinity of Wolf House Gallery suitable for leaving a car for several hours. If you wish to start the walk elsewhere, the best alternatives are Silverdale village, where there is parking on the shore, to start the walk at point 6, or Woodwell to start the walk at point 9.

THE WALK

1. Leave the car park by a path at the rear.

2. At a T junction with a cross path turn left and follow the broad path, ignoring all paths to the right. When the path forks, bear left then ignore a smaller path on the left to carry on along the main path to a tarmac lane.

Many wealthy families had permanent or summer residences in the area in the 19th century. Mrs Gaskell, referred to in the introduction, was just one. Those who came first could pick the best, south-facing sites with uninterrupted views. Those who came later sometimes interfered with the privacy of earlier residents to the extent that some owners were irritated enough to build high walls to ensure the continuing seclusion of their homes. These were called 'spite walls' and there is an example to the left of the path. It is easy to see where its height was increased.

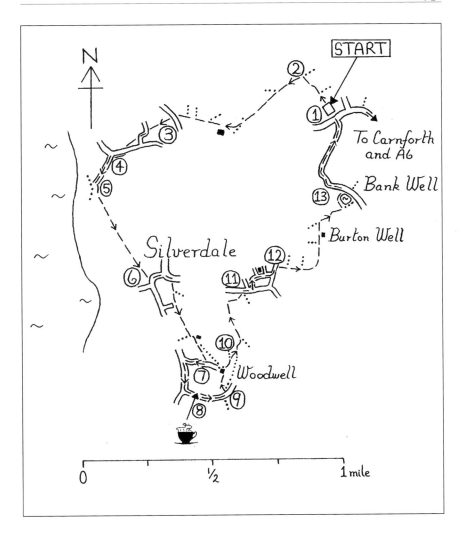

3. Take the track opposite, signed 'Cove Road' and join a lane at a bend. Walk along the lane for 20 yards then continue in the same direction along a path to Cove Road. Continue along the road, using the footpath on the left-hand side.

4. Take the first lane on the left, signed 'The Shore', and walk as far as a gate onto the foreshore.

5. At this point turn left on a path, signed 'The Lots', and follow it up to a wooden kissing gate and on across two fields to a road.

6. Turn left. At a T junction on a bend go ahead along Stankelt Road, signed 'Carnforth 4' for 25 yards then turn right on a public footpath along a track, signed 'Woodwell'. Carry on across the end of a lane through woods to a track. Turn left, then follow round to the right, past a cottage. Ignore a path on the left and continue with a wall on the left to a lane.

There has been a community here since time immemorial though the village as we see it today dates from the 19th century with few houses dating from before 1850. The river Kent regularly changes its course, swinging from the Silverdale side to Grange and back again. Local lore says it changes sides once in a person's lifetime. Early 20th century postcards show a pleasure steamer from Morecambe tied up at Silverdale, something that the expanses of salt marsh would have made impossible in more recent years. There are signs, however, that the channel is moving back towards Silverdale so perhaps we will once again see trips across the bay from Morecambe.

7. Turn right. At a T junction turn left then turn left at Hollins Lane to the teashop.

8. Turn left out of the teashop for 300 yards.

9. Go through a slit stile on the left and take the left-hand one of two paths (*), signed 'Woodwell', along the bottom of low limestone cliffs to a square, stone basin. This is Woodwell. Continue past the well and then up the cliffs. At the top turn left for 40 yards then fork right on an initially indistinct path across limestone pavement to a stile (**). The path that carries on along the top of the cliffs eventually fades out so if you think you have missed the fork, don't press on but retrace your steps.

(*) **Note:** The scramble up the cliffs is not at all difficult but if you would be happier not doing it, take the right-hand fork at the slit stile. This rejoins the route at the stile (**). However, you will not then pass Woodwell, one of the highlights of the walk.

Woodwell was one of the main wells serving Silverdale. The water emerges from the base of the cliff, is collected in a trough and runs into the large basin. If you look closely at the base of the cliff you can see a layer of impervious clay. This prevents the water seeping further through the rock so it emerges as a spring. This was a reliable, if inconvenient, source of water as the spring flows even in the driest weather. The water seeping out fell on the hills, the catchment area of the spring, many years before. As it percolates through the rock it dissolves some of the chemicals, making it extremely hard.

10. Go over the stile then bear right to a concrete post that has lost its signs. At this point turn left and follow the path on through woods, along the left-hand side of a field and along a walled track to a road.

11. Turn right then left along the second lane, The Green, after about 100 yards. Bear right at Crinkle Cottage, dated 1552, signed 'Burton Well via Bottoms Lane'. At a T junction turn left for 70 yards.

Crinkle Cottage does not date from 1552. When it was sold in 1952 the purchaser enquired about its age. He was told it was about 400 years old. Simple arithmetic suggested 1552 so he had a stone carved with that date and erected over the door. There may have been a house here in the 16th century, but it was not this one.

12. Turn right along a track, signed 'Public footpath Burton Well Lamberts Meadow' and follow it to Burton Well. Press on along the path, through a wooden kissing gate. At a cross path turn right to cross a footbridge over a stream. Go across the meadow then up a stepped path. Watch for a path on the left that leads down and round a pond to a lane.

Burton Well is similar to Woodwell and was the water supply for Silverdale Green. Some of the wells round Silverdale, including this one, used to have battling stones. These stones were used in the constant battle against dirt, to beat clothes clean. Lamberts Meadow is noticeably wet. This means the water is not draining away into the limestone as it does elsewhere. The reason is that the hollow in which it lies is lined with loess, a clayey soil blown in from Morecambe Bay during a drier geological era. The pond is known as Bank Well and was also used as a water supply. It seems to be a natural pond, also lined with loess. Left to themselves, ponds always get overgrown with vegetation and become first boggy ground and then dry land. A pond requires regular clearing if it is to remain open and this has recently been done at Bank Well, making an attractive spot.

13. Turn left and follow the lane back to the start.

Walk 2
LEIGHTON MOSS

*T*his is an outstanding walk in an outstanding corner of Lancashire and is greatly recommended. A high proportion of the route is through areas designated as being of special importance for conservation so it has a particular appeal for those interested in Nature. It includes the Royal Society for the Protection of Birds reserve at Leighton Moss – allow extra time if you enjoy bird watching. There is a public hide on the route overlooking open water with posters to help you identify what you see.

The Visitor Centre for Leighton Moss reserve is housed in a former barn and has interesting displays about the ecology of the area. Much of the top floor has been converted into a pleasant tea room so a visit is a must. The menu changes with the seasons but always includes a good selection of cakes, toasted teacakes and traditional hot puddings in winter. In keeping with the philosophy of the RSPB, they are keen to make the menu as organic and environmentally friendly as possible. Suggestions for lunch include sandwiches, for example dolphin friendly tuna, and daily specials such as Stilton and pear toastie. Everything is home-made and vegetarians are well catered for. It is open throughout the year between 10 am and 5 pm. Telephone: 01524 701601.

DISTANCE: 6 miles.

MAP: OS Landranger 97 Kendal and Morecambe.

STARTING POINT: Eaves Wood car park (GR 471759).

HOW TO GET THERE: From the traffic lights on the A6 in the centre of Carnforth take a road, signed 'Silverdale', past the station. On the outskirts of Warton turn left, signed 'Silverdale 3½'. Continue on the main road, over a level crossing and after a further ¼ mile turn right at a T junction. Pass Silverdale Station and take the next left, Park Road, to Eaves Wood car park after 100 yards on the right.

ALTERNATIVE STARTING POINT: If you wish to visit the teashop at the beginning or end of your walk, start at the RSPB Visitor Centre at Leighton Moss where there is ample parking in the car park across the road. The teashop is inside the Visitor Centre. You will then start the walk at point 14, turning right along the road out of the Visitor Centre.

THE WALK

1. Return to the road and turn left. At a T junction turn right for 90 yards.

2. Cross a stile on the left, signed 'Challan Hall'. Cross the railway and enter Gait Barrows National Nature Reserve. Go ahead across a field then bear left to a stile by a gate in front of buildings. Pass to the left of the buildings to a road.

3. Turn right for 90 yards then turn right again, signed 'Hawes Water Yealand Storrs' on a broad descending woodland path. Ignoring a path on the right across an open area and a path on the left, follow the path as it curves right round the top of Hawes Water. Soon after the path across the open area rejoins, bear left at a fork.

For a better view of the lake divert right off the main path at a small, derelict stone building. There are very few bodies of open water in this limestone country. Limestone is permeable and so water drains into the rock. As the glaciers retreated, debris was left and this formed a waterproof layer over the rock, allowing the lake to develop. Ponds and lakes are always temporary features of the landscape. As time goes by they are filled in with sediment carried by the streams that flow into the lake and by the accumulation of the skeletons of minute, single-celled organisms called

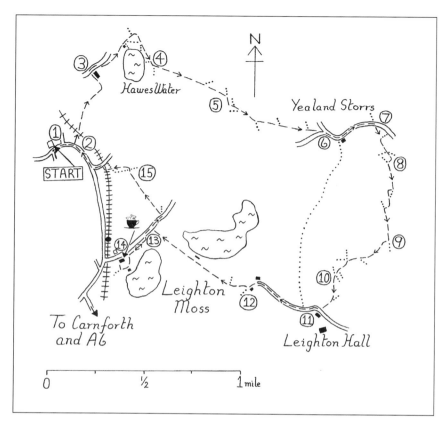

diatoms that live in the water. The white, gritty deposit that can be found in places round the edge was formed in this way. To the north and south are areas of flat land that was once under water. That to the north is called 'Clay Holes'. The clay, which allowed the lake to form, was used as the raw material for a small pottery industry that flourished in Silverdale in the Middle Ages. There was once a Little Hawes Water further up the valley. This has more or less completely disappeared and is just a boggy area except after heavy rain.

4. Some 90 yards after crossing a board walk over a marshy area go through a wooden kissing gate into a field. Bear diagonally right across the field to the remains of a stile in a tumbledown wall. Carry on in the same direction to a stile that challenges the well-nourished walker. Continue, still in the same direction, to another challenging stile, this time with a gate beside it.

5. Over the stile turn immediately right. Continue ahead as a more substantial path joins from the left and then one from the right for about ¹/₂ mile to emerge at a road junction.

6. Go ahead along Silverdale Road, signed 'Yealand Redmayne ¹/₂ Carnforth 4 Milnthorpe 5'. Walk past a footpath and some cottages on the right and continue for ¹/₄ mile.
    Note: The footpath on the right cuts across the fields to rejoin the route later. It saves about ³/₄ mile but misses one of the loveliest parts of the walk.

7. Turn right on a path signed 'Cringlebarrow Wood'. Join a wider path and continue uphill. At first the path is enclosed and then enters Cringlebarrow Wood at a field gate. Follow the path through the wood, ignoring all paths to right and left.

8. The path comes to a stile by a gate into a field. Do not cross the stile but turn right to walk round the field then uphill to a T junction. Turn left.

9. Turn right at a path signed 'Home Farm Leighton Hall'. Follow the path as it skirts Deepdale and ignore paths to the left. At a cross track turn left as directed by yellow arrows, the onward and right paths not being rights of way. Bear right when the track forks, again following the yellow arrows, to a gate into a field.

The limestone rock is eaten away here, forming caverns and passages. Deepdale was once a vast cave until the roof collapsed thousands of years ago. Photographs from the late 19th century show a round pond at the bottom, known as the Lily Pond. The slopes were not colonised by trees and it was an open and sunny spot. All this began to change in 1916 when a massive explosion tore through a munitions factory in Lancaster. The shock waves altered the drainage patterns in the limestone. The pond disappeared and the spring line in this area fell by 50 feet. St Catherine's Well at Leighton Hall, which was originally built on the spring line, dried up. All that is left of the Lily Pond today is a rather damp area colonised by willows.

10. Bear slightly left to a gate and continue to a second gate onto a lane at a farm.

Built of very white limestone and sitting in a bowl of tree-framed pasture, Leighton Hall is one of Lancashire's most attractive stately homes. There has been a house here since the 13th century. In 1715 the owner was Albert Hodgson, a staunch Catholic as so many were in Lancashire. He took part in the Jacobite rebellion and was captured at Preston. The Government soldiers sacked and burned the Tudor building and it had to be rebuilt. The present aspect of Leighton Hall is a testament to the power of fashion. The Georgian building had its appearance altered in 1825 to the then fashionable neo-Gothic style and the tower and cross-wing were added in 1870 to create an in vogue asymmetrical façade. Since the early 19th century the house and estate have belonged to the Gillow family, of furniture fame, and their descendants. There is an exceptional collection of Gillow furniture in the house, which is open on some summer afternoons. Telephone: 01524 734474.

11. Turn right and pass the point where the short cut from point 6 rejoins the main route. After Grisedale Farm the lane becomes a track. Continue for 80 yards to a stone barn on the left.

12. Turn right at this point, which soon leads to the causeway across Leighton Moss to a road.

There is more about the reserve on the information boards and at the Visitor Centre, which also houses the welcome tea room.

13. Turn left to the teashop in the RSPB Visitor Centre. After 100 yards, walking on the road can be avoided by using a permissive path on the left, which dogs are not permitted to use. Don't go too far along this path; turn right 40 yards after Lilian's Hide to the Visitor Centre and the tea room upstairs.

14. Return to the point where the causeway joins the road and carry on along the road for a further 160 yards to where two paths leave on the left. Walk in the direction of the left-hand path, signed 'Redbridge': the line across the field is shown by posts and is initially along a faint track that soon fades completely. Follow the line to a stile in the far right corner and on across a golf course to a stile 20 yards to the right of a gate into a wood.

15. Cross a track 20 yards into the wood and continue on a narrow path. Recross the track and go ahead over the railway. Turn right and walk up the edge of a field to a wooden kissing gate onto a lane. Turn left. At the main road turn right, back to the start.

Walk 3
CROOK-O'-LUNE AND CATON

The Lune has claims to be Lancashire's loveliest river and the Crook-o'-Lune is rated among its most idyllic stretches. The route starts beside the river and high above it at the car park for the popular Crook-o'-Lune picnic site. There are excellent views of the river, flowing in its tranquil valley. Most of the outward route is beside the river as it makes a broad meander before returning on a permissive path along the level track of a disused railway, calling in at Caton for refreshment. This is a highly recommended walk for its unsurpassed river scenery and it is almost completely level.

The Cottage in Caton is housed in an ancient building, dated 1692 over the door. It is an outstanding traditional teashop and restaurant, which offers some interesting twists on traditional fare. For a light lunch there are filled baguettes with tempting suggestions such as poached salmon with lemon and dill mayonnaise or the bookmaker – strips of sirloin with onion rings. The baked potatoes are similarly enterprising and include Brie and bacon with sour cream or creamy garlic mushrooms with crispy bacon. The daily specials include both light meals such as deep fried black pudding with tomato chutney and full meals such as lamb and peach pie. There is a range of unbelievably sinful gateaux, temptingly displayed in a sweet cabinet and other teatime goodies including Danish pastries and teacakes are served. Cream teas are available. As well as the attractive interior, there are several tables on a patio in front of the building. It is open every day except Monday throughout the year (open bank holidays), from noon on Tuesday and Sunday, 11 am on Wednesday, Thursday and Friday, and from 10 am on Saturday. The Cottage remains open for early evening meals and until 9 pm on Saturday. Telephone: 01524 770833.

DISTANCE: 4 miles.

MAP: OS Landranger 97 Kendal and Morecambe or Outdoor Leisure 41 Forest of Bowland and Ribblesdale.

STARTING POINT: Crook-o'-Lune Picnic Site car park, (GR 521647).

HOW TO GET THERE: From the A683 Lancaster–Kirkby Lonsdale road, 2 miles east of junction 34 on the M6, take a minor road signed 'Halton' and 'Crook-o'-Lune Picnic Site'. Cross the river to a car park on the right.

ALTERNATIVE STARTING POINT: If you wish to visit the teashop at the beginning or end of your walk, start in Caton where there is a small public car park (four hours limited parking) in Station Road. Turn right along the main road to the teashop on the right. You will then start the walk at point 5.

THE WALK

The Lune rises in Yorkshire but is nonetheless one of Lancashire's foremost rivers. At the Crook-o'-Lune it makes a loop round a bluff that blocks its otherwise lazy passage to the sea. The early travellers liked a good view just as much as we do today and the view from Crook-o'-Lune was highly rated. Wordsworth, in his 'Guide to the Lakes', recommended lengthening the journey from Lancaster to Kendal by eight miles to enjoy the prospect. One visitor was the artist Turner, who came here in 1818 and made many sketches and studies as the basis of a famous watercolour.

1. Facing the road, go down some steps on the left of the car park and follow the path down to the river bank. Walk upstream, with the river Lune on your right. Continue through a wood. As you emerge from the wood, bear slightly left to cross a tributary at a footbridge and then go ahead to an aqueduct over the Lune.

These woods are a particular delight in spring when they are carpeted by flowers including wild garlic, bluebells and wood anemones. The composition of woodland

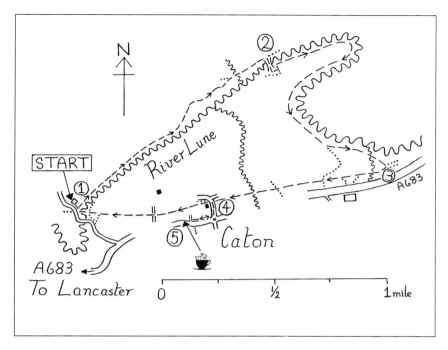

can be clearly seen from the path. There are basically four layers of vegetation - the canopy of the trees, the shrubs such as hazel and holly, the field layer including the flowers and the ground layer of lichens and mosses. In our temperate climate most trees are deciduous, losing their leaves in the winter. Once the leaves emerge in spring, it is not long before the canopy becomes too dense for enough light to penetrate. The flowers of the field layer have to make the most of the brief period between the weather becoming warm enough to sustain plant growth and the canopy closing over. This is why woodland is carpeted with flowers in spring, which have all but disappeared by high summer. The plants of the ground layer need to get growing as fast as possible in the spring. They therefore have a store of food in swollen, underground stems and leaves - a bulb. Most of the bulbs we plant for spring colour in our gardens started as woodland plants.

2. Cross the river, using the aqueduct walkway, and turn left to continue upriver. The path eventually becomes a track. When the track bends right, away from the river, carry on upstream.

3. Some 80 yards after crossing a small tributary go over a stile on the right and up to a permissive path on the course of a disused

The river Lune.

railway. Turn right and follow the path over two tracks.

Incompetence is no new phenomenon, as the story of this railway demonstrates! It was built in 1849 from Lancaster to Wennington. The original rolling stock was built to the wrong specification: it was too wide, too low and too heavy. The route was never a success. It was taken over by Midland Railway and then became part of London Midland Scottish. It finally fell to the Beeching axe in 1966.

4. At the third track turn left into Caton, passing Station House. At a main road turn right to the teashop on the right.

The monks of Furness Abbey, who also had a farm or grange nearby owned the fishing rights on the Lune, noted for its salmon. The monks sold surplus fish from fish stones at the base of the old gnarled tree at the entrance to The Croft, by the Ship Inn. The tree is said to be a Druid's Oak, but that is a bit of modern whimsy. Though the tree is obviously old it is by no means as old as the druids, themselves more the product of modern imagination than well documented history.

5. Retrace your steps to the path along the disused railway and turn left to continue along it for ¹/₂ mile, back to the start.

22

Walk 4
CLOUGHA PIKE

*T*his is undoubtedly the most challenging walk in this book but the ascent to the 1,356 feet of Clougha Pike rewards the walker with unparalleled views over north-west Lancashire and beyond to the Lake District and Yorkshire Dales. The climb itself is not arduous. Taken steadily with much admiring of the ever expanding views, it is well within the capacity of most ramblers. The route then wends across the top to Grit Fell before descending to the viewpoint at Jubilee Tower. The route then returns round the hill, still with outstanding scenery spread before you, and passes an excellent teashop just when you need it most! This walk demands a clear day as its main interest lies in the splendid panoramas to be enjoyed and in misty conditions route finding may not be so easy.

Clougha Pike is an access area by agreement with Lancashire County Council. Dogs are not allowed and access may be limited during the grouse shooting season starting 12 August.

The Tea Room at Brow Top Craft Centre, near Quernmore, is housed in a converted 17th century barn. The cakes are delicious and there are also moreish scones served with cream. Substantial meals are available, including a sustaining Farm House Fry-Up or Cumberland sausage and egg and chips. For a lighter appetite sandwiches are also on offer and there is a special children's menu. The Tea Room is attractively decorated in pine with exposed stonework and beams and there are also a couple of tables outside from which to enjoy the views. Above the Tea Room is an interesting craft gallery, a treasure trove of wares all produced in the locality. Brow Top is open until 5.30 pm every day in summer, opening at 10.30 am from Monday to Saturday and 12.30 pm on Sunday. In winter it closes on Wednesday. Telephone: 01524 66833.

DISTANCE: 7 miles

MAP: OS Landranger 102 Preston and Blackpool and 97 Kendal and Morecambe or Outdoor Leisure 41 Forest of Bowland and Ribblesdale.

STARTING POINT: Birk Bank car park for Clougha Pike Access Area (GR 526604).

HOW TO GET THERE: To find the starting place from the south start from the A6 one mile south of junction 33 on the M6 and take a minor road north-east, signed 'Quernmore 6'. After 1/4 mile turn right, signed 'Abbeystead 5 Caton 9 Quernmore'. Take the next left, Whams Lane at Station House, signed 'Quernmore Caton'. Continue on this road for 4 miles, crossing a more major road. At Quernmore village crossroads continue ahead, signed 'Caton' on Rigg Lane for just under 1/2 mile. Turn right on a single track, unsigned lane for 1/2 mile to a car park on the right. This is easily missed, as it is not signed from the lane.

From the north take a minor road, signed 'Quernmore 31/2 Trough of Bowland 21/2', from the A683, the Lancaster-Kirkby Lonsdale road, at the western end of Caton. After 2 miles turn left, signed 'Quernmore 2 Bay Horse 6'. Half a mile after a church on the right turn left on a single track, unsigned lane and continue to the car park, as above.

ALTERNATIVE STARTING POINT: If you wish to visit the teashop at the beginning or end of your walk, there is a car park at Brow Top Craft Centre where the teashop is housed but permission must be sought before leaving a car for a long period. You will then start the walk at point 11.

THE WALK

Note: The first part of the route is through wild country and the path can be wet and boggy, so the wise walker will go prepared.

1. Take a path through a gate at the rear of the car park. When it

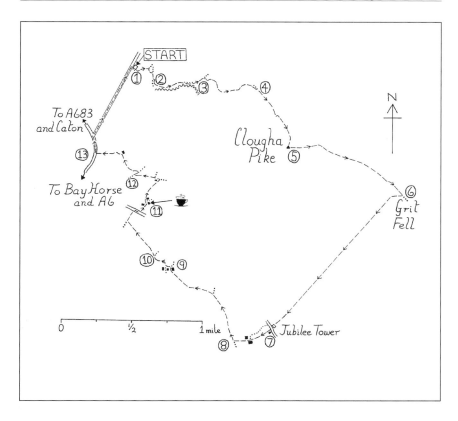

forks after about 200 yards, bear right to a T junction with a cross path. Turn right as far as a gate across the path, signed 'Strictly Private'.

2. Turn left onto a board walk across a boggy area and when this finishes, continue on the path, initially with a wall on the right and then a stream. After passing through a glade of trees, the path becomes obscure for a while but stick close to the stream on the right and you will soon pick it up again. When it fragments into smaller paths, press on up the hill, heading to the right of a rocky outcrop, to find two ladder stiles over walls.

3. Go over the stile on the right. This hill is Little Windy Clough and you will sometimes be uncomfortably aware of how it got its name! It can also be very wet underfoot hereabouts. Climb initially with a wall on the left and then bear right to the end of a wall. Clougha Pike can now be seen ahead. Walk towards it with a wall on your left to a small gate. Through the gate follow the path slightly left to meet a wall on the ridge.

4. Turn right alongside the wall. When the wall ends at a rocky outcrop, scramble up to continue on the path along the ridge to the trig point – and a possibly welcome windbreak – on the top of Clougha Pike.

5. After enjoying the stupendous views, stand at the trig point with your back to Lancaster below and take the path ahead; in effect, you have turned left from your previous direction. Press on along the path over the flat moor top, crossing a stile over a fence. The path is mostly quite clear and marked by occasional cairns. Cross a second stile and walk with a fence on the left to a fence junction with a ladder stile and posts with maps of the access area. This is the highest point of the route at about 1,530 feet and is just below the top of the flat expanse of the summit of Grit Fell.

This area is part of the Forest of Bowland, designated as an Area of Outstanding Natural Beauty in 1964. The moors seem so wild and untouched it is hard to believe this is a man-made landscape produced by grazing and management for grouse. Without human interference, these hills would be covered in forest. This was part of the lands of the Saxon Earl Tostig. It was good hunting country and soon taken over by the Normans after the Conquest. Only the King and his favourites could hunt here. There were draconian forest laws and those who broke them were tried at Slaidburn (see Walk 20). Hunting, in a way, is still an important part of local life. The Forest of Bowland boasts some of Britain's finest grouse moors. Red grouse is only found in Britain and cannot be reared artificially. Heather is burned on a rotation system to provide a patchwork of young growth for feeding and older stands for nesting cover. The moors have few public footpaths. Some parts, such as this, have been opened up to walkers by Access Agreements negotiated between the owners and Lancashire County Council. The Clougha Access Area is the largest, covering 1,717 acres.

6. Do not cross the stile but turn right to walk with the fence on the left down to a car park and road.

7. Cross the road and take a signed path next to Jubilee Tower to a farm track. Follow the surfaced track past farm buildings.

8. Immediately after crossing a cattle grid, as the track bends sharp left, turn right over a stile marked by an inset stone with a carving of a bird. Walk along the right hand side of three fields. In the fourth field head just to the right of the farm seen ahead to find a stile over a fence. Now head down to the left of a large round structure – in fact, a slurry store – to pick up a track.

9. Walk along the track through a ford and past buildings.

10. Immediately after a sharp right hand bend cross a stile next to a field gate on the left. Walk beside a row of hawthorns. When these end, continue ahead, bearing slightly right, down to a gate onto a surfaced track in the far right corner of the field. Turn right to a road then right again for 100 yards to Brow Top Crafts and Teas on the left.

11. Turn right out of the teashop. Pass to the left of a barn to a gate then immediately through the left hand one of two gates to walk along the right hand side of a field. Go over a stile into a second field and cross it to a stile just to the right of a house. Over the stile go by the house to a surfaced drive. Follow the drive downhill to a track on the right.

12. Turn sharp right, crossing a cattle grid, signed 'Rooten Brook Farm'. After 80 yards turn left on a track that leads downhill along the top edge of a thickly wooded valley and eventually emerges in a field. Go ahead down by a wall onto a drive at Old Mill House. Walk along the drive to a road.

13. Turn right for 300 yards then bear right along a lane to the car park where the walk started.

Walk 5
SCORTON

The highlight of this walk is undoubtedly the stretch through the steep-sided Grize Dale valley. Its sylvan charms are complemented by a small reservoir and the first ¹/₄ mile is a mass of rhododendrons in season. The route starts near the M6 but it soon leaves behind the persistent rumble as it wends its way by quiet field paths and lanes – one with a ford – to Grize Dale. It is not far from there to the ancient village of Scorton and its famous teashop. Suitably refreshed, there is a short waterside stroll back to the start.

The Priory in Scorton is a large and well-known establishment popular with walkers and cyclists as well as the tea drinkers of Lancashire. It serves everything from an all-day breakfast through full meals to tasty sandwiches. The teatime staples of scones and toasted teacakes are supplemented by a selection of cakes and gateaux, accompanied by a choice of speciality teas. There are some tables outside. It is open between 9 am and 9.30 pm throughout the year. Telephone: 01524 791255.

DISTANCE: 5½ miles.

MAP: OS Landranger 102 Preston and Blackpool or Outdoor Leisure 41 Forest of Bowland and Ribblesdale.

STARTING POINT: Scorton Picnic Site at Cleveley Bridge (GR 504503).

HOW TO GET THERE: From the A6 about 3 miles north of Garstang take a minor road signed 'Hollins Lane Dolphinholme'. Take the first lane on the right, Cleveley Bank Lane, and continue along it for about a mile, ignoring a lane on the left, to Scorton Picnic Site on the left.

ALTERNATIVE STARTING POINT: If you wish to visit the teashop at the beginning or end of your walk, start in Scorton where there is limited street parking. The teashop is in the middle of the village. You will then start the walk at point 10.

THE WALK

1. Return to the lane and turn left. Walk over the M6 and turn left at a T junction.

2. Turn right on a little lane in front of the entrance to Cliftons Farm. After 135 yards turn left over a stile on a signed path. At the time of writing this is not visible on the ground but leads across a field to a stile onto a track just to the left of farm buildings.

3. Turn right through the farmyard, following the arrows, to emerge in a field. Walk up the left hand side of the field and across a second field to a stile in the far left corner. Over the stile bear slightly right to a tricky double gate into another farmyard. Walk through the farmyard to a lane.

4. Turn right. Cross a ford at a footbridge and continue until the lane ends at a metal field gate. Continue in the same direction along a track, signed 'Public Bridlepath to Grize Dale and Nicky Nook'. Continue for about 1½ miles, passing Grize Dale reservoir.

5. Watch for a footbridge over the river. At this point turn right on a footpath signed 'Higher Lane ¼m' and follow the clear path to a lane.

6. Turn right for 175 yards then go over a stile on the left. Head down a field to a stile on the right then across to a stile into an enclosure round a small brick building and over another stile onto a drive. Turn right over a cattle grid to a lane.

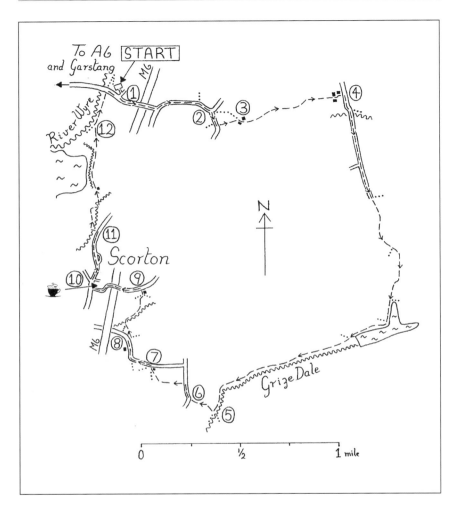

7. Turn left.

8. Some 100 yards after Tithe Barn Cottage turn right over a ladder stile and immediately turn left to find a kissing gate into a wood on the right. Follow the path down some steps and across a footbridge then through a wood to another wooden kissing gate into a field. Bear right to a further kissing gate by a stone cottage. Go ahead to a lane.

Grize Dale.

At this point in the walk, it is only a short distance to Scorton, which means 'enclosure with long incision' and refers to the gorge the route has just crossed.

9. Turn left over the M6 into Scorton to the teashop on the right.

Scorton is an attractive village and has been designated a conservation area. It has three churches C of E, Catholic and Methodist – and no pub!

10. From the teashop turn right and follow the main road, signed 'Scorton Picnic Site Trough of Bowland', out of the village for about 1/4 mile.

11. Take a footpath on the left, signed 'Cleveley Bridge', as it crosses and recrosses Park Brook. The path passes to the left of a dilapidated corrugated iron barn then bears left onto a slight bank with another stream now on the left. Follow the path to a stile giving onto a track.

12. Turn right along the track. At a lane turn right, back to the car park where the walk started.

Walk 6
GARSTANG

Undemanding, yet full of interest and variety, this route is highly recommended. It explores the countryside around Garstang, one of Lancashire's oldest towns, which is visited en route. There is plenty of waterside walking, with stretches by both the river Wyre and the Lancaster Canal. The towpath has fine views of both the Fylde to the west and the Bleasdale Fells to the east. As well as bustling Garstang and its waterways, the walk passes a spring reputed to have medicinal powers, a ruined castle, water management systems and transport arteries old and new.

Sitting on an important route north, Garstang has long made a business of catering for the weary traveller. The Court Tea Room continues this tradition admirably. It occupies an airy, modern building in one of Garstang's alleys or weines. A good selection of cakes is offered, but I advise organising your day to have lunch there, if possible. The menu features innovative and delicious toasties such as ciabatta with garlic butter, roast pepper, mushrooms and tomato topped with melted cheese. Alternatives include salads, stuffed jacket potatoes and sandwiches, which you can enjoy with home-made soup. Court Tea Room is open between 10 am and 4.30 pm throughout the year except on Sunday and is closed on Wednesday afternoon in winter. Telephone: 01995 602541.

DISTANCE: 5 miles.

MAP: OS Landranger 102 Preston and Blackpool or Outdoor Leisure 41 Forest of Bowland and Ribblesdale.

STARTING POINT: Parking area near Barnacre church (GR 512460).

HOW TO GET THERE: From the A6 Preston–Lancaster road, 2½ miles north of its junction with the A586, take a minor road signed 'Scorton 1½ Trough of Bowland'. Just over a bridge turn right, signed 'Barnacre Calder Vale 4 Oakenclough 4'. Follow the lane over the M6 to a large, informal parking area on the left just before Barnacre church.

ALTERNATIVE STARTING POINT: If you wish to visit the teashop at the beginning or end of your walk, start in Garstang where there is ample parking in a car park by the Council offices. This is pay and display during the week but is free on Sundays. Go to the far side of the car park to the river and turn right on the riverside path to pick up the walk at point 7.

THE WALK

1. Facing the lane turn left for 40 yards, as far as a post box. Turn left down some steps and onto a footbridge. Over the bridge turn left to a stile. Cross the stile and head slightly right, skirting to the right of a large depression, which is a disused quarry and now a home to rabbits. Now go downhill beside a fence to a stile.

2. Over the stile turn right beside a fence for about 30 yards to reach a huge tree with a divided trunk. After passing the tree, bear left across to a stile onto a track. Turn left along the track to a gate onto a lane.

This massive and venerable tree is an alder. Just beneath the tree is a spring, reputed to have medicinal properties. Members of the Hamilton family used to bathe here and a stone spa was constructed. Much of the stonework has now collapsed but its original square form can be made out. The water still flows freely and it is known as Lady Hamilton's Well.

3. Turn right.

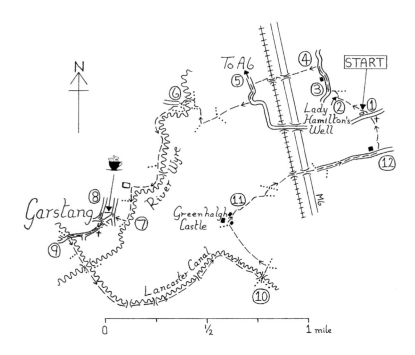

4. Some 125 yards after passing Crosby Cottage on the left, turn left over a stile. Head along the right hand side of a field to a footbridge over the M6 then on to a second footbridge over the railway. Carry on along the right hand side of a field to a lane.

5. Turn left. When the lane turns sharp left, turn right on a signed path along an unsurfaced track. Continue ahead at a junction with a farm track on the left and footpath on the right. When the track bends left to a ford, continue ahead to a wooden gate beside a field gate and follow the path to a footbridge over the river. The gracious stone bridge a short way upriver carries an aqueduct. Go over the footbridge and along the path to rejoin the track as it emerges from the ford. Turn right along the track for 40 yards.

6. Turn left through a pedestrian gate. Through the gate turn right to a sculpture of a dipper and the river bank. Turn right beside the river and follow the path past flood defences and as it skirts a playing field to a car park in Garstang. Continue by the river past the car park.

7. Take the second path on the right to emerge in the centre of Garstang by the Market Cross. Turn right then left along Thomas's Weine to the teashop.

Garstang's heyday was in the 18th century when it was an important staging post for both mail and passenger coaches on the main road north, now the A6. At one time there were seven inns providing stabling for horses and refreshment to weary passengers. Prosperity increased still further when the canal came in 1797. The third transport artery to come this way, the railway, passed by Garstang. Perhaps that is one reason why the town is so attractive today. It has remained a human place with many individual shops. It has a wealth of old buildings and several alleys. Similar alleys are found in Kendal and Penrith. When marauding Scots came raiding cattle, sheep and people could be gathered into them for safety. Edward II granted a market charter in 1310 but as time went by the market fell into abeyance. It restarted in 1679 and the Thursday market has been part of the life of Garstang ever since. The Market Cross is on the site of the original market and dates from 1752, when the original was replaced.

8. Turn right out of the teashop. At a road turn left, take the first left then the next right to shortly pass St Thomas's church on the left. Continue as far as a bridge over a canal.

9. Cross the bridge and take a path on the left down to the towpath. Turn right to walk with the canal on your left. Continue beside the canal to the fifth bridge, number 56.

This area between the fells to the east and the sea to the west has always been an important arterial route and this is as true today as it was five hundred years ago. The mode of transport may change but the route does not. On this walk we have seen the latest – the M6 with all its noise and pollution – as well as the railway, still the main west coast line to the north. The canal, the earliest manifestation, seems altogether more environmentally friendly today, though we might not have thought so if we had passed this way when it was being built or in full use. The Lancaster Canal was built in the closing years of the 18th century. Designed by John Rennie it has 41 miles without locks, achieved by following contours. It crosses an attractive single span aqueduct over the river Wyre. One of the most important services in its commercial days was the fast fly boats pulled by relays of horses changed every five or six miles. Passengers made the journey from Preston to Kendal in seven hours. Some 30 to 40 people were carried in two classes with refreshments served en route. To begin with, they competed with the railway but ultimately lost out to the railway's greater speed.

10. Go up to a track and turn left over the canal. A few yards after passing through a gate across the track and before passing beneath power cables turn left over a stile. Head across a field to pick up a track leading to a farm. Pass the farmhouse then turn right on a track that leads past farm buildings to a field gate with a stile beside it.

The Stanley family backed the winning side in one of the most significant battles in English history. They supported Henry Tudor (Henry VII) against Richard Plantagenet (Richard III) at the Battle of Bosworth in 1485. Thomas Stanley was made first Earl of Derby and placed the crown on Henry's head. Part of his reward was extensive lands in this part of Lancashire and permission to construct a fortified castle. By 1490 Greenhalgh Castle had been built with towers 60 feet high and overlooking Garstang and its important bridge over the river Wyre. The Stanleys chose the wrong side in the next major conflict when they supported the King in the Civil War. As one of the last Royalist strongholds to surrender to the Parliamentary troops, it was extensively slighted: in other words, virtually pulled down so it couldn't be used again. The stones provided a ready source of material for local farmers and the adjacent Castle Farm is mainly built of reused stone.

11. Over the stile turn left along an increasingly faint track to a stile on the left. Cross the stile and a small field to another stile. Go down into a cutting of a disused railway and up the other side. Press on across a field, slightly right, to first a bridge over the railway and then one across the motorway. Continue ahead along a lane leading from the bridge.

12. Turn left on a signed path just after Clarkson's Farm. Head along the left hand side of a field for 55 yards then cross a concrete footbridge and stile on the left into a farmyard. Over the stile turn right to continue in the same direction. When the track fades out in a field press on along the right hand side of the field to a stile onto a short path to a lane. Turn left, back to the start.

The small church at Barnacre is surprisingly modern, having been built in this somewhat isolated position in 1912 by the local landowner. It is usually locked.

Walk 7
PILLING

The Fylde air is like wine, guaranteed to buck you up. That is just one of the reasons for the success of the Fylde coast resorts across the Wyre estuary. This short, level walk is a world away from them and is ideal for blowing away any cobwebs. It wends its easy way by quiet lanes and field paths to Pilling and its teashop. The climax, and what makes this walk so special for most of the year (see note at point 7) is the last half mile of the return along Pilling bank. There are tremendous wide views across Morecambe Bay with, on a clear day, the hills of Cumbria beyond. This area is of international importance for wildfowl so don't forget your binoculars if you are interested in birds.

Old Carr Farm in Pilling serves an excellent selection of cakes and pies, temptingly displayed, including a proper Lancashire custard. The full afternoon tea includes sandwiches and scones, as well as cakes. A substantial breakfast is offered and this isn't just for early birds as it is served all day. For lunch there are filled jacket potatoes, sandwiches and salads and for bigger appetites, the menu offers a range of full meals, mostly with chips. You can enjoy your refreshment indoors, in a pleasant conservatory or on the patio by the plants for sale. Old Carr Farm is open between 10 am and 5.30 pm every day except Thursday (closed in December). Telephone: 01253 790249.

When the teashop is closed the pub in Pilling, The Golden Ball, serves food.

DISTANCE: 4 miles.
MAP: OS Landranger 102 Preston and Blackpool.
STARTING POINT: Lane Ends car park (GR 416493).
HOW TO GET THERE: From the A588 between Poulton-le-Fylde and Lancaster, 4 miles south of Cockerham, take a minor road signed 'Lane Ends Amenity Area' to a car park on the right.
ALTERNATIVE STARTING POINT: If you wish to visit the teashop at the beginning or end of your walk, start in Pilling where there is ample parking in the village car park. You will then start the walk at point 6.

THE WALK

1. Return to the road and turn left to a T junction. Turn right.

2. At the next road junction turn left along Horse Park Lane, signed 'Garstang'. Walk along this quiet lane for the best part of a mile, passing an unusually large duck pond with many disputatious inhabitants.

3. Opposite a lane on the left, turn right over a stile on a signed path along the left hand side of a narrow field. At the opposite side do not cross a stile but turn right along the edge of this field and the left hand side of the next two fields to reach a stile giving on to a fenced path. Follow the path a few yards to another stile.

4. Over the stile turn left along the left hand side of a field to a further stile. Immediately over the stile turn right and follow the path to cross two footbridges into a field. Turn left along the edge of the field to a road.

5. Turn left for 30 yards then right on a footpath along a track. When this shortly ends, go over a stile ahead into a field and bear slightly left to a footbridge. Over the bridge bear slightly right to a second footbridge with a stout wooden barrier to be climbed, then go ahead to a gate onto a track. Walk along the track into Pilling and the teashop on the left.

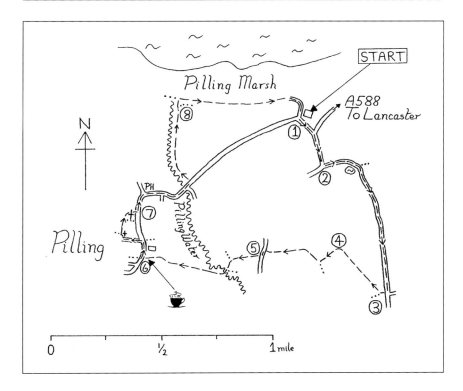

Pilling stands on relatively firm land about 20 feet above sea level astride Pilling Water, which sluggishly carries moss drainage into Morecambe Bay. There has been a community here among the swamps of the moss since Bronze Age times when a unique road made of timber was constructed, locally known as Kate's Pad. The Over Wyre mosses were the last to be drained and for most of its history Pilling has been unusually isolated: it is hardly at the centre of affairs today!

6. From the teashop turn right along the road through the village. Turn left along a surfaced track immediately before the Old Ship. Turn right into the graveyard and pass to the left of the church. Continue on the path to the new church then turn right to return to the road.

The Old Ship started life as a gentleman's residence, built in 1782 by George Dickson, a slave trader. It is said to be haunted by a lady dressed in Georgian clothes with a worried look on her face.

When a new church was built in 1877, the old one, erected in 1710, was left standing. It is kept locked, though if you want to see inside a notice tells you where to collect the key. Its main interest is a previous incumbent who made an enormous contribution to science and navigation. George Holden was vicar between 1758 and 1767. He was ideally placed to study tides and his contribution was the invention of tide tables, still in universal use today. A sundial over the door of the old church is dedicated to his memory.

7. Turn left and walk out of the village and over the river to a road junction. Bear left, signed 'Lancaster', for 50 yards then turn left along a track.

Note: The public are not allowed to use the permissive path along the embankment between Boxing Day and Good Friday. This is to protect over-wintering birds and sheep during the lambing season. Between these dates, continue along the lane back to the start. Dogs are not allowed on the embankment at any time so please continue along the lane if you have a dog with you.

8. Just before the track bends sharp right, bear left up onto the sea defences. Turn right, back to the start.

Constructed by North West Water in 1981, the embankment was designed to protect Pilling and the surrounding prime agricultural land from periodic inundation by the sea. The views across Morecambe Bay are outstanding. The only blot is the large, boxy structure, which is Heysham Nuclear Power Station. When the tide is out, an enormous expanse of sand is exposed. This may look like a barren waste to us but, just below the surface of the sand, it is heaving with life. For example, the population of Baltic tellin, a shellfish with a pinkish or white shell up to about 2 cm. long, has been estimated at 5,000 per square metre. This richness supports a huge population of birds and this habitat is of international importance. For that reason it is a Site of Special Scientific Interest and managed by English Nature. Some species are using Morecambe Bay as a refuelling stop on their long journey from their breeding grounds in the far north to the over-wintering sites further south. Others, such as pink-footed geese, come from further north to spend the winter here while some, for example dunlin, are year round residents. When the tide is out, the birds forage out on the sands and then roost on the surrounding salt marsh when the tide comes in. Some 160 species have been recorded here.

Walk 8
LITTLE AND GREAT ECCLESTON

The Fylde is the rectangle of land between the river Ribble, the river Wyre, the coast and the Bleasdale Fells. It comes from the Saxon word for field, which tells you how flat it is and so this walk is level and undemanding. The circuit starts and finishes along the banks of the river Wyre. Even though the river still has ten miles to flow to the sea at Fleetwood, it is tidal here. Earth banks have been constructed to protect the fields from a tidal surge and these make for particularly easy walking. If you can possibly time your walk for high tide, the river is much prettier. The route leaves the river to make its way by quiet lanes and field paths to the thriving village of Great Eccleston, which boasts an excellent tea shop, before returning to the banks of the Wyre for the final stretch.

 Charlotte's is a deservedly popular traditional teashop. It uses charming blue and white china, for sale in the gift shop with which it shares premises. For a light lunch there are attractively presented open sandwiches such as roast beef and red onion or ham with cheese and apple coleslaw. More substantially there is quiche of the day served with salad and crusty bread or a country platter of ham, pâté and cheese or Charlotte's platter with salmon, prawns and smoked salmon. The toasted sandwiches are very popular. The sweet temptations range from traditional cakes including lemon cake or warm ginger cake with cream to traditional puddings such as jam roly-poly and Christmas pudding all year – very sustaining on a cold winter's day! There are some seriously sinful temptations such as chocolate torte with orange segments and banoffi nut meringue. Charlotte's is open on Monday to Saturday from 10 am. until 5 pm and on Sunday from 11 am to 5 pm throughout the year. Telephone: 01995 671108.

DISTANCE: 4 miles.

MAP: OS Landranger 102 Preston and Blackpool.

STARTING POINT: Cartford Bridge (GR 422408).

HOW TO GET THERE: From the A586 Blackpool–Garstang road take a minor road, Blackpool Old Road, signed 'Pilling 6 Little Eccleston'. Turn down Cartford Lane, signed 'Pilling' towards Cartford Bridge and park on the right as you approach the bridge and pub. There are several spots where you can leave a car without causing inconvenience.

ALTERNATIVE STARTING POINT: If you wish to visit the teashop at the beginning or end of your walk, start in Great Eccleston where there is some street parking but avoid Wednesday, market day. The teashop is in the centre of the village. You will then start the walk at point 5.

THE WALK

The hamlet of Little Eccleston grew up at the site of a ford across the river Wyre. The bridge that replaced the ford is one of the few toll bridges where you still have to pay to cross. The Cartford Hotel, now a popular pub and restaurant, is reputed to be haunted by ghosts who move things around and switch lights on and off . . .

1. Walk down the road towards the bridge. Immediately before the bridge turn left on a riverside path, shortly walking on a raised causeway. Follow the path on the embankment as it bears left away from the river, now walking beside a small tidal creek to the main road.

2. Turn left on a path beside the road for 100 yards then turn right along a lane so minor it is closed to traffic except for access. When the lane forks at Little Eccleston Hall, bear left.

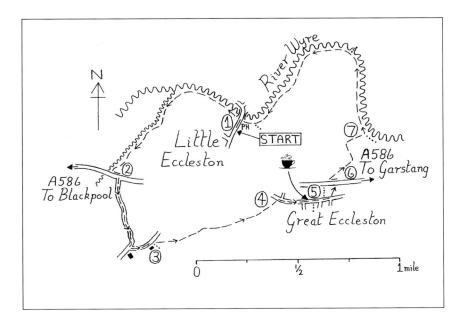

Little Eccleston Hall belonged to the quaintly named ffrance family. It is little altered and is now a farm. Thomas Robert Wilson ffrance built Cartford Bridge in 1831. His wife became terrified of crossing the river after two servant girls fell in the water and narrowly escaped drowning.

3. Immediately after a modern thatched house on the right, two paths leave the road on the right. Take the one that bears diagonally left across a field to a stile by a gate in the far left corner – it is not visible on the ground at the time of writing. Go diagonally left over the next field to another stile. Now continue along the right hand side of a small field and over a stile onto a short stretch of hedged path. Carry on along the right hand side of a further field, more hedged path and a track to a road.

4. Turn right into Great Eccleston and the teashop on the left in the square.

In the Domesday Book the village is called 'Eglestun', which means the place of the church. This is surprising, for in the modern Great Eccleston the church is some distance from the village centre and the building apparently dates from the 18th century. There is no record of a Saxon church so perhaps the name actually has some other derivation. In the past Great Eccleston was called 'Little London' by Fylde people because of its sparkling social life as one of the most important centres in the area. The Wednesday market in the square is very popular and is a modern innovation: it started in 1974 following a campaign by the Parish Council. The Agricultural Show, founded in 1853 and still a major event, also took place in the square until 1939.

5. Turn left out of the teashop and continue through the village. Take an unnamed lane on the left, opposite Barrows Lane, to the main road.

6. Cross the road and turn left for 30 yards to a stile by a gate. Go over the stile and ahead for 15 yards to a public footpath fingerpost. The right of way skirts right round a field to a stile by a gate in the far left corner. Over the stile turn right to a second stile leading up the embankment beside the river.

The river Wyre is tidal as far as St Michael's three miles upstream. The embankment is to protect the surrounding fields from flooding.

7. Turn left along the embankment, back to Cartford Bridge.

Walk 9
WORDEN PARK

This walk is a saunter across the fields to Leyland's Worden Park. The scenery is unspectacular, but very appealing. The well-kept hedges are studded with fine mature trees and the paths are quiet. It is an attractive short walk at any time of year but I like it best in spring when the hay meadows are full of flowers, the hedges dressed with blossom and the rhododendrons in Worden Park are in bloom. There is an entertaining opportunity to exercise your route finding skills as the walk passes the entrance to a fiendish maze in Worden Park so, if you haven't worked up an appetite, you can wander around for ages trying to find your way in and – even more difficult – out again!

Worden Park Coffee Shop in the Arts and Crafts Centre offers an outstanding selection of sandwiches on ciabatta, rosemary focaccia or traditional crusty bread. The delicious fillings include such suggestions as smoked turkey with apple and cranberry, Brie with kiwi fruit and walnuts or pastrami with onion and mustard. For a hot meal there is Cumberland sausage with herb and onion mash as well as daily specials. To tempt a sweet tooth there are desserts such as caramel, pecan and chocolate tart with chocolate sauce and cream or ice cream as well as tempting cakes. Various teas and coffees are served and, particularly welcome on a winter's day, hot chocolate with whipped cream and a chocolate flake. It is attractively housed in former stables with tables in the former stalls and there are some tables outside in a woodland setting as well. Open every day throughout the year from 11 am, the closing time depends on the season and the weather and can be between 3.30 pm on a wet day in winter and 6 pm on a fine day in summer. Telephone: 01772 623329.

DISTANCE: 3½ miles.

MAP: OS Landranger 108 Liverpool and 102 Preston and Blackpool.

STARTING POINT: Runshaw Moor (GR 541198).

HOW TO GET THERE: From the A49 Preston–Wigan road at Euxton, 1 mile north of its junction with the A581 take a minor road west called Runshaw Lane. After 1 mile, just after Runshaw Hall Road on the right, park in a small, informal layby on the left.

ALTERNATIVE STARTING POINT: If you wish to visit the teashop at the beginning or end of your walk, start in the car park by the Arts and Craft Centre in Worden Park. The teashop is through an arch in a wall. You will then start the walk at point 8.

THE WALK

1. Facing the road, turn left (west) and walk as far as the Plough. Continue for a further 100 yards.

2. Turn right on a path along the entrance to Bournes Farm. Go through the farmyard and ahead over a stile to the right of two metal gates onto a track, initially between hedges and then on the right-hand side of a field. At the end of the field, ignore a path on the left and continue ahead across a field, now on a path. Over a stile by a gate on the far side, bear diagonally left to a stile in the far corner. Walk along the right hand side of a field towards a farm to find a stile onto a track.

3. Turn right for 50 yards. Immediately before the track forks turn left to walk with a wire fence on the left to a stile giving onto a surfaced drive. Turn right to a lane.

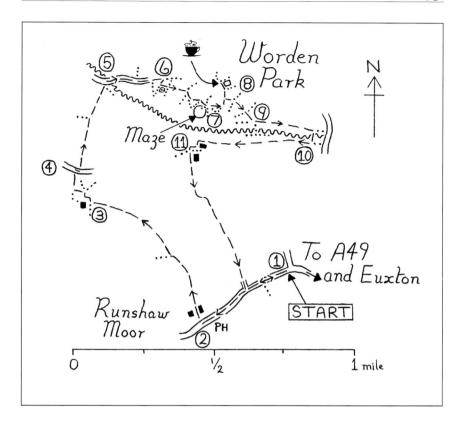

4. Turn right again for 30 yards then left on a path, signed 'Shawbrook Road ½'. Walk with a hedge on the left. When this ends go ahead for 40 yards to a gap in a hedge and on along the left-hand side of a second field to a stile ahead. Over the stile go ahead across a field to a stone slab over a ditch and a stile in the right hand corner. Now proceed along the left-hand side of two fields to a stile by a gate onto a lane.

5. Turn right, immediately crossing a small river and continue until you pass through white metal gates into Worden Park.

For 300 years the oddly named ffarington family lived in Worden Hall set in some 150 acres of parkland. Worden Hall was destroyed by fire in 1941 and the estate was eventually bought for the people of Leyland.

6. Some 40 yards into the park, just by a Worden Park sign, turn right on a gravel path for 10 yards then left on an unmade path to the left of a pond. Press ahead in the same direction through the wood, ignoring all paths to left and right. When a metal fence ahead bars the way, bear right round a service area then on in the same direction, soon on a path past the maze. Follow this round to the right. A path on the right leads to the maze entrance.

Beware! In my opinion, it is much more fiendish than the famous one at Hampton Court so do not venture in unless you have some time to spare and are confident of your navigation skills.

☕ **7.** At the maze exit, guarded by six ft high stone obelisks, turn left into a formal garden. At the far end turn left again, past a knot garden to a car park and the teashop.

8. From the teashop retrace your steps across the car park to the knot garden. Turn left through white wrought iron gates on a surfaced path. After some 50 yards take the second of two paths on the right, which descends into a valley.

9. At a cross path turn left to walk with a stream on the right. As a gate and road come into view, some 45 yards after a bench, turn right through trees to find a bridge over the stream you have been walking beside. (If you arrive at a road, you have missed the path by 100 yards.)

10. Over the bridge turn right to walk with the stream on your right along the right hand side of several fields. Eventually, the stream veers away and the path heads across a field to a stile to the right of farm buildings. Over the stile turn left and walk round a field to a stile by a gate on the left.

11. Now take a surfaced track ahead, passing barns on the left. The slight elevation of this point gives some splendid views across the West Lancashire moss to the Irish Sea beyond. Follow the track to a road and turn left, back to the starting point. (If you started the walk at the teashop, turn right.)

Walk 10
CROSTON

A subtitle for this route could be 'The Two Rivers Walk', as it includes a path by the river Lostock before tea and the Yarrow afterwards. It is a very easy walk with no more than 20 feet of ascent the whole way. It explores the area round Croston, one of the oldest communities in this part of West Lancashire. The village has a charming centre, with ancient packhorse bridge, historic church and a village green overlooked by a teashop.

Memory Lane Tea Rooms shares premises with a gift shop in a building that once housed the local Co-op and has an engaging ambience. A selection of cakes is available and an unusual suggestion is a cream tea for two. For a light lunch there is a choice of sandwiches, toasted if you wish, filled jacket potatoes or salads and a tasty soup of the day. The teapots are particularly capacious and a top-up is freely offered. They are open throughout the year except on Mondays (open Bank Holiday Mondays) between 11 am and 4 pm. Telephone: 01772 601927.

DISTANCE: 4 miles.

MAP: OS Landranger 108 Liverpool.

STARTING POINT: Informal layby on the south side of the B5249 some 100 yards west of its junction with the A581 (GR 503190).

HOW TO GET THERE: From the A581 Chorley–Croston road take the B5249 for about 100 yards towards Bretherton to an informal layby on the left.

ALTERNATIVE STARTING POINT: If you wish to visit the teashop at the beginning or end of your walk, start in Croston where there is a small car park by the village green, across the road from the teashop. You will then start the walk at point 5.

THE WALK

Across the road from the start is the Royal Umpire Caravan Site in the grounds of Gradwell Farm. It takes its name from a museum that was once here. Its prize exhibit was the Royal Liverpool Umpire Stagecoach, which ran from Liverpool to London about 150 years ago. The farmhouse was originally the home of the Gradwell family. They were devout Roman Catholics and several sons went into the priesthood. Many priests found refuge here when Catholics were persecuted. The garden has a stone cross that commemorates one Father Winkley, who was chaplain to the Gradwell family. A young girl in white is said to have haunted the farm, of which more later . . .

1. Cross the road to the entrance to Mill Hotel and immediately turn left on a track into the caravan site rally field. Walk along the track until it bends right then go ahead through a gate and ahead across a field to meet a river.

2. Turn left to walk with the river on your right to a lane. Cross the lane and head diagonally left across a field, in the line shown by a sign, to a stile. Over the stile walk up the left hand side of a first field and the right hand side of a second to a road.

3. Turn right for 200 yards to a signed path on the left. Follow the clear, surfaced path, bearing right at a fork.

4. When the path reaches a road, turn immediately left over a ladder stile into a field. Cross the field diagonally right, then turn right on a fenced path that leads onto a playing field. Skirt right round the playing field to a road. Turn left to the teashop on the right.

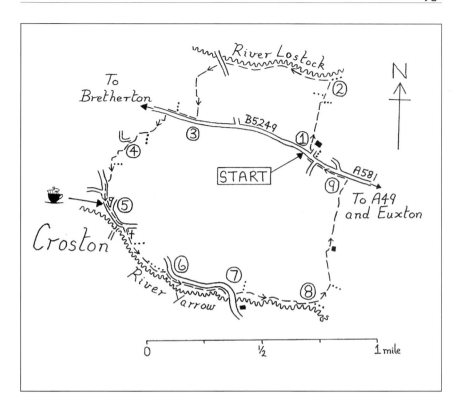

The centre of Croston is particularly attractive with stone and brick cottages on one side of the road and the river Yarrow, here confined between walls, on the other. The river is spanned by a narrow, arched sandstone packhorse bridge bearing the date 1682. The cross at the top of Church Street is probably not the original, from which the town takes its name. Indeed, the head only dates from 1953 and was carved from a mill-stone. The base is much older. Celtic missionaries of St Aidan built a church on the site of St Michael and All Angels, though the present building is 16th century and only a Norman door remains of older buildings. To the east of the church is the impressive Old Rectory, widely considered one of the finest Georgian buildings in the north of England. John of Gaunt founded a school here in 1372. James Hyett, then Vicar of Croston, gave it an endowment in 1660. He had Puritan sympathies and was later forced from the living for refusing to obey the Act of Uniformity that, among other requirements unacceptable to those of his persuasion, demanded the use of the revised Anglican prayer book. He died in Preston in 1663 and is commemorated by a plaque.

5. Turn right out of the teashop. Turn right along Church Street. Bear right round the church to pick up a path by a river behind the building. Carry on by the river to a lane.

6. Turn right for ¼ mile.

7. Immediately before a bridge over the river, turn left on a path signed 'Highfield Road ½ Eccleston 1½'. The path starts along a track. As the track bends left, go over a stile on the right to continue by the river for about ¼ mile.

8. Watch for a couple of plank bridges over ditches on the left, just before a metal field gate. Cross the bridges then strike diagonally left across a field to the left hand one of two metal gates. Go through the gate and walk along an increasingly obvious track past a farm and up to a road.

The track passes Sarscow Farm. Legend has it that a girl who lived here fell passionately in love with Father Winkley, chaplain at Gradwell Farm. When he succumbed to a fever and died, the grief-stricken girl took her own life by throwing herself down a forty foot well. Her restless spirit was said to haunt Gradwell Farm and made itself known by the sound of feminine footsteps on the stairs, rustling skirts and jolting beds. Her most bizarre appearance was in the late 1950s. The Southport bus screeched to a halt outside Gradwell Farm. The shaken driver was convinced a girl in white had appeared in front of the bus and he had run over her. Fearing the worst, he went to investigate but nothing was there ... The lovelorn ghost of the 'Sarscow Lady' has not been seen since the cross commemorating Father Winkley was moved from the orchard to the garden of Gradwell Farm some years ago.

9. Turn left, back to the start.

Walk 11
HAIGH HALL

The stretch of the Leeds and Liverpool Canal explored on this walk contours round a hillside overlooking the Douglas valley. This means there are wide ranging views from the towpath that forms much of the outward leg of this very pleasant walk. The route then leads into Haigh Country Park and through its woodland and gardens to the teashop in the old stable block. The return is easy – all level or downhill. The entirety of this circuit is on well-made paths or tracks and there are no stiles to navigate; a determined person could take a pushchair round. You will be surprised to find such an attractive walk so near the heart of industrial Lancashire and I urge you to enjoy it.

The Stables Cafeteria at Haigh Country Park is housed in the stable block of Haigh Hall, which also contains craft displays, an information centre, shop and toilets. Tall windows overlook an enclosed courtyard with some tables outside. There are lots of Lancashire things with chips as well as filled jacket potatoes and tasty and well-filled sandwiches. Unfortunately, the tea does not come in pots but the cakes are good and service at the self-service counter is unbelievably efficient as well as friendly and helpful. While you eat, it is interesting to read the newspaper account of the visit of the Prince and Princess of Wales to Wigan and Haigh Hall in June 1873 when, we are told, the people of Lancashire had never enjoyed such prosperity. The Stables is open all year from 9.30 am to 5 pm in summer and from 10 am to 4.30 pm between October and Easter. The shop sells a wide selection of old fashioned sweets such as aniseed balls, cinder toffee and winter nips from the jar. Telephone: 01942 832895.

DISTANCE: 4 miles.

MAP: OS Landranger 108 Liverpool and 109 Manchester.

STARTING POINT: Canalside parking by the Crawford Arms on the Leeds and Liverpool Canal and the B5239, Red Rock Lane, (GR 584099).

HOW TO GET THERE: From the A5106 Standish–Chorley road take the B5239 eastwards, Red Rock Lane, signed 'Haigh Hall', to the Crawford Arms on the right.

ALTERNATIVE STARTING POINT: If you wish to visit the teashop at the beginning or end of your walk, start in the Pay and Display car park at Haigh Hall. The teashop is by the car park. You will then start the walk at point 5.

THE WALK

1. With your back to the road and the Crawford Arms on the right, walk along the towpath for about 1½ miles to the third bridge over the canal, number 60.

The Leeds and Liverpool Canal is 121 miles long, making it Britain's longest. It links Leeds and Liverpool by way of Wigan, Chorley, Blackburn, Burnley, Skipton and Bradford and to do this climbs over the Pennines using 91 locks. It was authorised by Parliament in 1770 and cost £1.2 million, taking over 40 years to build and finally opening in 1816. The Earls of Crawford, who owned Haigh Hall at that time, had substantial mining interests and bought 33 boats to use on the canal. It was a major freight route for over 100 years but by the early 1960s this had virtually finished. It is now extensively used for recreation.

2. Bear right from the towpath up to a surfaced drive and turn left across the bridge over the canal.

3. As the drive bends right, turn left on a broad path. Continue across a drive and a miniature railway track. Ignore all paths and

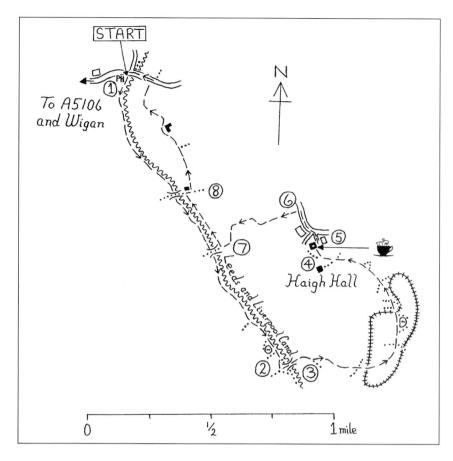

tracks to right and left and pass to the left of a pond. The path eventually becomes surfaced; press on past the crazy golf and an ornamental pond.

After the Norman Conquest the manor of Haigh was owned by the Norreys family and by 1295 was the property of an heiress, Mabel Norreys. She married Sir William Bradshaigh (or Bradshaw). He was, somewhat mysteriously, away from Haigh between 1315 and 1322. In his absence, his wife, Mabel, was persuaded to marry a Welsh knight. In those days, the term did not mean literally someone from Wales but was applied to any foreigner. On his return in 1322, Sir William is said to have mingled with the villagers, disguised as a palmer – a pilgrim returning from the Holy Land. Lady Mabel noticed the man and how much he resembled her

supposedly dead husband. Sir William made himself known and the usurper fled, hotly pursued by Sir William, who was never slow to protect his interests. Sir William caught up with him and killed him near Newton-le-Willows. Lady Mabel was instructed by her confessor to walk barefoot and barelegged, carrying a taper, once a week from Haigh to Standishgate in Wigan. The cross then became known as Mab's Cross.

 4. Bear right through a play area to the teashop.

The Bradshaigh family continued to own Haigh down the centuries. They were involved in mining, particularly cannel coal. This is an unusual form of coal. It is clean to the touch and can be carved so it was used to make ornaments and trinkets. There was even a summerhouse made from cannel in the 17th century, which was still in existence in the early 19th century when Sir Walter Scott visited Haigh. He was much taken with the tale of Mabel and William and used the story in 'The Betrothed'.

5. From the teashop turn left and go round the building, past the car park to a lane. Turn left.

In 1770 a ten-year-old girl inherited Haigh. When she grew up she married Alexander Lindsay, 23rd Earl of Crawford. Their son, James, built the present Haigh Hall. The work started about 1830 and took nearly twenty years. Earl James was a practical man, interested in engineering, and the hall is full of his inventions. For example, the inside doors have special hinges that lets them swing open and then be locked open by a twist of the handle. The Hall was at the height of luxury when the Prince and Princess of Wales visited in 1873. It was filled with fine furniture and precious objects. When the visit of royalty was arranged, the whole hall was redecorated with new carpets and curtains at a cost of £80,000. The royal apartments were open for three days after the visitors left at sixpence a time.

6. Turn left on a track marked by a block of stone with a footprint. Follow this down to the canal at a bridge.

7. Do not cross the canal but turn right to walk on the opposite bank to the outward leg as far as the next bridge.

8. Turn right along a track for 50 yards then turn left on a track by Pendlebury House for 1/2 mile, continuing ahead as it passes a large house and then becomes its drive. At a road turn left, back to the start.

Walk 12
ANGLEZARKE AND RIVINGTON

*H*ard by Bolton, Horwich and Chorley and not far from the industrial giant of Manchester, Anglezarke has been exploited for water, stone and lead. These incursions have been softened by time and Nature to make the attractive and varied landscape explored on this walk. There is much woodland walking on the way to the teashop in Rivington village. The route wends its way between the maze of reservoirs for which this area is famous and there are also attractive paths by the rivers and streams that feed them. If you enjoy walking by water, this route should figure high on your list.

 The Village Green Tea Room is housed in an old chapel. It is attractively decorated in traditional style. The tasty and substantial food includes sustaining soup, sandwiches and filled jacket potatoes. Full lunches are also served between 11.30 am and 2 pm and breakfast is available all day. To satisfy a sweet tooth there are tempting cakes, custards and scones served the traditional way with jam and cream. The Village

Green Tea Room has several innovative ideas such as crumpets by candlelight in darkest winter and a pianist to serenade you on Sunday. Open on Tuesday to Friday from 10.30 am until 4 pm and from 9.30 am until 5 pm at the weekends. Telephone: 01257 271669.

DISTANCE: 5 miles.

MAP: OS Landranger 109 Manchester or Explorer 19 West Pennine Moors.

STARTING POINT: Anglezarke car park. (GR 620161).

HOW TO GET THERE: From the A673 Chorley–Horwich road, at some traffic lights by the Ridgeway Arms in Adlington, turn along Babylon Lane. At a road junction at the Bay Horse, turn right over the M61 and take the next left, signed 'Anglezarke' for 1½ miles to Anglezarke car park on the left.

ALTERNATIVE STARTING POINT: If you wish to visit the teashop at the beginning or end of your walk, start in Rivington village where there is ample parking by Rivington school. Turn right through the village to the teashop. You will then start the walk at point 10.

THE WALK

1. With your back to the entrance drive, go to the lower left side of the car park to find a substantial wooden kissing gate, signed 'Anglezarke Trail'. Follow the main, surfaced path and continue ahead as another surfaced path joins from the left. Keep on through a disused quarry and down towards Anglezarke Reservoir.

The quarry was worked in the 19th and early 20th centuries. The hard, coarse-grained sandstone was taken by cart to Adlington and thence by train to Manchester, where many roads were built of Anglezarke stone. It was also much used in the construction of the many reservoirs hereabouts. Today it is a wonderful illustration of the recuperative powers of Nature with the slopes clothed in heather, bilberry and gorse.

2. At a T junction with a surfaced track turn right alongside the reservoir and follow the track as it starts to climb as far as a pronounced right hand bend.

3. Leave the surfaced track to walk on a woodland path that starts between a notice illustrating birds you might see and a wooden bench. Ignore a path on the left giving anglers access to the reservoir and continue ahead, signed 'Woodland Trail', soon passing a bench well placed to admire the view. Follow the path round the hillside above the reservoir then down to a cross path. Go ahead on a clear

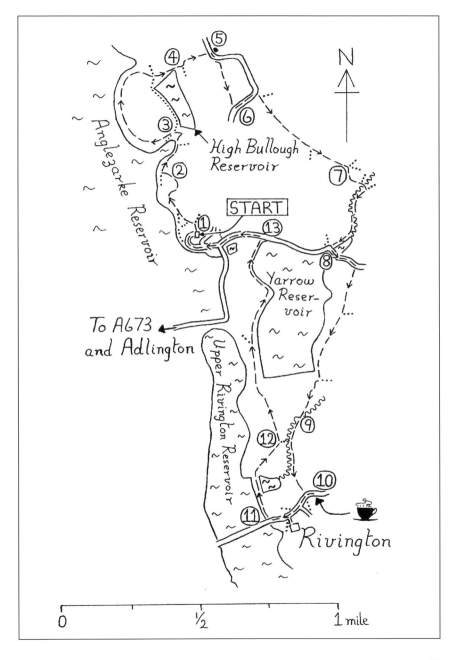

N

④

⑤

③

~

~

~

Anglezarke Reservoir

②

High Bullough
Reservoir

⑥

⑦

①

START

⑬

⑧

Yarrow
Reser-
voir

To A673
and Adlington

Upper Rivington Reservoir

⑨

⑫

⑩

⑪

Rivington

0   ½   1 mile

but unsigned path that climbs up the other side of the valley.

4. At the end of the reservoir on the right, continue ahead, signed 'Manor House Farm'. As you climb and emerge from the wood, your efforts are rewarded with extensive views behind so you have every excuse to stop and admire them frequently. Go across a small field to emerge on a lane opposite Manor House.

5. Turn right for 45 yards. Go through some gates on the right and immediately bear left through a gate across a small paddock to a stile. Over the stile go along the right hand side of a field to another stile then continue in the same direction to a prominent ladder stile over a wall onto a lane.

6. Turn left. When the lane bends left, turn right on a public bridleway along a track for $\frac{1}{2}$ mile.

7. The track approaches a gate with a stile on its **right**. Do not cross the stile but turn right downhill on a clear path with a wire fence on the left and marked with a blue arrow. (**N.B.** Do not confuse this with an earlier, somewhat similar path just after a gate with a stile on its **left** and marked with a yellow arrow. Follow the path down into a thickly wooded valley – Lead Mines Clough – and across a stream to meet a cross track. Turn right to a road.

Millions of years ago hot liquid rich in lead rose from deep within the Earth's crust and flowed into fissures and faults in the rock here. As it cooled and solidified, the lead was deposited as galena or lead ore. This was first mined where visible near the surface and then the miners dug into the hillside to win the valuable ore. The conical depressions on the hillside to the left of the path are where shafts have collapsed. The spoil was dumped on the hillside and can still be seen – it is barely colonised by vegetation as the lead it contains is toxic to plants. Fragments of silvery-grey galena can be found among the spoil, produced when the rock was crushed to release the galena. The earliest record of lead mining here dates from 1692, though the deposits were certainly worked earlier, and it continued intermittently until the 1830s. The shafts were filled in during the Depression of the 1930s to provide work for the unemployed people of Chorley.

8. Turn left over a reservoir and walk along the road for some 200 yards. Near the top of the hill cross a stile on the right and walk across a field. Follow the path as it contours round the hillside above the reservoir. Though it is only intermittently visible, it is not difficult to follow as it is waymarked with yellow arrows. After the end of the reservoir, the path descends to a stile and then joins a track.

9. At the end of an avenue of magnificent trees, go through a gate across the track and after 10 yards cross a stile on the left to continue along the left hand bank of a stream. Stay on the obvious path up some steps to a lane in Rivington. Turn left to the teashop.

Clustered round the village green with its stocks, Rivington is a gem. One of the most attractive buildings is the Unitarian chapel, built in 1703 and little changed since that time. In 1662 the incumbent of Rivington church, Samuel Newton, was expelled from the Church for refusing to accept the Book of Common Prayer and he and his followers built the chapel, one of the oldest Nonconformist places of worship in Lancashire.

10. Turn left out of the teashop. Bear right at a road junction, signed 'Adlington and Chorley'.

James Pilkington was a son of the local landowners and became Protestant Bishop of Durham. An ardent Protestant, he destroyed many cathedral treasures he deemed tinged with Popery. He was equally keen on education and founded Rivington Grammar School, passed on the left, in 1566. In summer the pupils worked from 6 am until 6 pm with a two-hour break; in winter their school hours were from sunrise to sunset – not a regime that would find favour with today's students. The secondary pupils combined with those from nearby Blackrod in 1873 and the school has since catered for children of primary age.

11. Immediately before the road passes between Upper and Lower Rivington Reservoirs, turn right on a track signed 'Yarrow Reservoir'.

12. Just before the track enters a wood and starts to descend, turn left on a public bridleway along a track. When it forks after 1/2 mile, continue ahead on the right branch.

13. At a road turn left. At a road junction turn right, signed 'Anglezarke 3/4 Heapey 31/4', back to Anglezarke car park and the start.

Walk 13
LEVER PARK

*L*ancashire has produced many men of energy and enterprise but none
with a stronger philanthropic streak than William Hesketh Lever, later Lord
Leverhulme, son of a grocer from Bolton, who became a soap magnate. He
bought part of the Rivington estate in 1900 and made all but 45 acres
available for the recreation of local people. It still admirably fulfils that
function today. This walk has something for everyone and in particular
appeals to children. Many features of the gardens that Lord Leverhulme laid
out remain as romantic ruins that children – and their elders – can freely
explore. There is also a ruined castle, which is not all it seems to be!

 There is a teashop in Great House Barn, which is Saxon in origin
though much restored. It has offered refreshment stops for over half a
century and is very popular. Be sure to look up at the enormous cruck
frame constructed of solid oak. A selection of tempting cakes is offered and
scones are available. For lunch you will find soup of the day, sandwiches,

baguettes and filled jacket potatoes. Open from 10.30 am to 5 pm every day throughout the year. Telephone: 01204 697738.

DISTANCE: 3½ miles.
MAP: OS Landranger 109 Manchester or Explorer 19 West Pennine Moors.
STARTING POINT: Car park on Lever Park Road, Horwich. (GR 635128).
HOW TO GET THERE: From the A673, the Chorley–Horwich road, on the northern outskirts of Horwich, take Lever Park Road, between two stone obelisks and signed 'Rivington', for ½ mile to the first car park on the left, just after the speed derestriction sign.
ALTERNATIVE STARTING POINT: If you wish to visit the teashop at the beginning or end of your walk, start in Great House car park by the teashop. You will then start the walk at point 7.

THE WALK
1. Return to the road and turn left for 120 yards then right on a signed bridleway up to a major cross track.

Bolton's greatest son must be William Hesketh Lever. He was a man of great enterprise, energy and philanthropy. Born in 1851 the son of a Bolton grocer, he started the soap company that made his fortune in 1884. It soon outgrew the original premises in Wigan and Lever bought a site on the Wirral bank of the Mersey where he developed a new factory and a model village, Port Sunlight, for the workers. He pioneered the eight-hour working day and staff canteens. Any of his other achievements would be enough for one person! He was Mayor of Bolton and Liberal MP for Wirral, bought Lancaster House in London and gave it to the nation, sponsored Schools of Architecture, Russian Studies and Tropical Medicine, founded MacFisheries to promote fish sales – and so the list goes on. He was happily married to his childhood sweetheart whom he met at infant school: when he became a baronet, he took the name Lord Leverhulme by joining his name to his wife's maiden name. His life is a model of what one man can achieve and he always claimed his success came 'through plodding hard work within the reach of all who will make the necessary sacrifice.'

2. Turn left for 50 yards then sharp right on a path protected by three wooden posts. Follow this up to another major track.

3. Turn left through a gate across the track. When the track forks, bear right to continue up through a gate into a wood. Ignore all paths to left and right for about ½ mile until you come to an information board on the right.

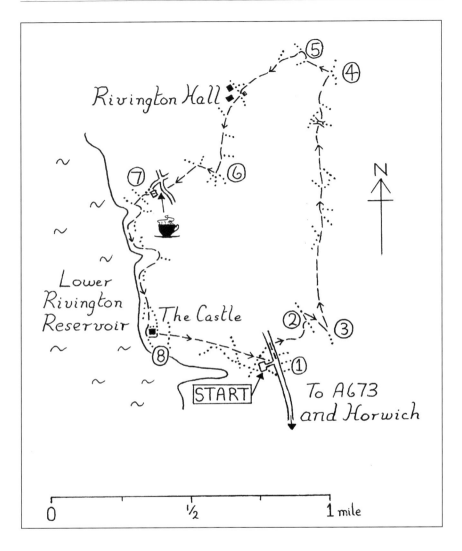

Rivington Hall

Lower
Rivington
Reservoir

The Castle

START

To A673
and Horwich

N

0   ½   1 mile

On the 45 acres of the Rivington estate that he reserved for his own use, Lever built a
large wooden bungalow called 'Royton Cottage'. In the grounds he created a
fantasy of caves, waterfalls, bridges and hanging gardens. In July 1913, while he
and his wife were dining with the King and Queen at Knowsley as guests of the Earl
and Countess of Derby, a suffragette, Edith Rigby, bumped a can of paraffin up the
hill and burned the house down. Three weeks later his wife died. The house was

rebuilt of more durable materials and a circular ballroom was added. After Lord Leverhulme's death in 1925, the house and gardens fell into disrepair and the gardens became overgrown. The house was demolished in 1947. In recent years some restoration work has been carried out on the gardens, and they are fascinating to explore. The paths on the right lead into the gardens and the bridge across the track was designed by Lord Leverhulme himself.

4. Turn left down six steps to a stile then follow the path down to a fenced track.

5. Turn right then bear left to follow the fence round to the left. As the track approaches buildings, bear left to pass in front of a house. Now bear left again then immediately right to continue in more or less the same direction to a complex path and track junction.

6. Turn right for 130 yards then turn left on a smaller path through trees to emerge on a road opposite the teashop.

7. From the rear of the car park behind the teashop take a path ahead towards a reservoir. At a cross path in front of a wooden fence turn left. When the fence ends continue by the reservoir to eventually join a more substantial path coming in from the left. Press on in the same direction round a wildlife conservation area. Bear right at a fork, back to the reservoir. The path soon divides into several parallel paths. Keep ahead on any of these as far as a large stone structure to the left overlooking the reservoir. This is Liverpool Castle.

Rivington Reservoir is one of a chain built in the middle of the 19th century to supply water to the growing city of Liverpool. Lord Leverhulme planned that most of the land he had bought should be made freely available to local people for recreation. Liverpool Corporation opposed the proposal. They were concerned about the impact of the plan on the catchment area. Liverpool Corporation definitely came second in the dispute! When the dust had settled, Lord Leverhulme emerged with compensation amounting to double his original purchase price. He got to keep the area planned for his own use and 400 acres, known as Lever Park, were to be set aside for public enjoyment. Liverpool Castle is a replica of the structure that for 500 years dominated the centre of Liverpool. Lord Leverhulme built it in acknowledgement of his Merseyside connections.

8. Climb up beside the castle and take a broad path leading from the entrance gate to the car park on the right where this walk started.

Walk 14
TURTON

This is a fascinating short walk crammed with historic and wildlife interest. It makes use of the well-constructed paths in the Country Park round Jumbles Reservoir and ventures beyond to an attractive village and one of Lancashire's most interesting historic houses with its welcome tea room. All in all, this route is outstanding and I heartily recommend it to you.

 Turton Tower Tea Room is in the kitchen of the house. It is an attractive setting with the old Victorian range, exposed beams and very thick walls. Alternatively, tea can be enjoyed in the garden overlooking a tennis court where an All England champion once practised. The menu includes a selection of sandwiches and cakes and there are scones and cream as well. Lancashire County Council manages Turton Tower and the tea room is accessible without paying to visit the house. However, it is well worth a visit and the tea room is also accessible from the reception and small shop. It is open from early February until late November except on Thursdays and Fridays (open on Thursdays between May and September). It is always open in the afternoon until 4 pm but sometimes in the morning and sometimes later – ring to check. Telephone: 01204 852203.

☕ On summer afternoons, Jumbles Tea Garden in the information centre by the car park also serves refreshments. Sandwiches and hot snacks are available as well as scones with jam and cream and toasted tea bread. All the seating is out of doors, overlooking the reservoir.

When the teashops are closed the Chetham Arms in Chapeltown, passed en route, serves food.

DISTANCE: 4 miles.
MAP: OS Landranger 109 Manchester or Explorer 19 West Pennine Moors.
STARTING POINT: Jumbles Country Park car park (GR 736139).
HOW TO GET THERE: Jumbles Country Park is signed from the A676 between Bolton and Ramsbottom.
ALTERNATIVE STARTING POINT: If you wish to visit Turton Tower Tea Room at the beginning or end of your walk, there is a large car park nearby reached from the B6391. You will then start the walk at point 7.

The walk

1. Cross the access road to the car park and go ahead on a path past the information centre to walk with the reservoir on your left. Look for monsters in the trees on the left. As the reservoir narrows, pass a bridge on the left and continue up the valley, now by a river.

2. Cross the river at a stone bridge by some modern houses and walk along a cobbled track. When the cobbles end, turn left on a path up to a road.

3. Turn left for 75 yards then right uphill on a cobbled path starting over a stile. Walk up to a gate and continue past the former St Anne's school, now a private house. Go through a gate on the right into Chapeltown churchyard. Pass to the right of the church and halfway along the building, turn right to a gate out of the churchyard.

4. Turn left opposite a gate onto a football pitch on the right. At a main road turn right then almost immediately left along Kay Street, next to the Chetham Arms. Carry on along a track after the pub car park to a T junction with a cobbled track.

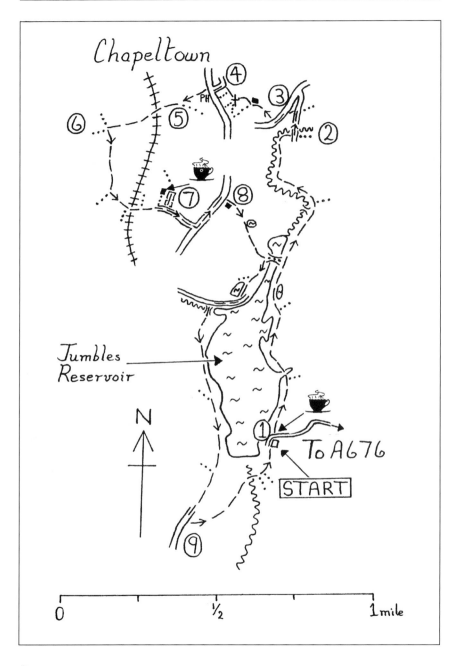

5. Turn right. Cross a railway line and bear left to a metal gate beside a field gate. Be sure not to leave it open. At the time of writing, a sign threatens you with a fine of £1,000 if you transgress! Through the gate bear left to walk with a wall on the left up to a gate and cross track.

☕ **6.** Turn left and keep on the track as it bends left downhill. Recross the railway at an elaborate, turreted bridge and carry on to the entrance to Turton Tower on the left. Turn left through the parking areas and past the main entrance to reach the tea room on the left.

The house has evolved from a defensive pele tower built about 1400 by the Torboc family. It gave protection against both raiding Scots and their relations, with whom they were always feuding. Down the centuries it underwent constant modification as fashions came and went. The last private owners were the Kays. John Charles Kay was a keen sportsman and won the All England Mixed Doubles in 1889 and 1891. Now owned by Lancashire County Council, it is well worth a visit and the excellent booklet explains its history and evolution. Tel: 01204 852203.

7. Return through the car park and turn left along the track – now a surfaced entrance drive – to a road. Turn left.

8. Just before a left hand bend turn right over a stile on a signed path past a pill-box. Follow the clear path over the brow of a hill and down into woodland to a bridge over the reservoir. Do not be surprised if it looks familiar: it is one passed on the other side earlier in the walk. Do not cross the bridge but turn right on a path beside the reservoir. Pass a car park and at an access road turn right for 140 yards. Now turn left over a bridge to continue round the reservoir. Continue when the path eventually becomes a broad track shaded by lime trees.

9. Turn left through a gate on a footpath signed 'Jumbles Reservoir ³/₄km'. Follow the path down to a bridge over a river and up steps on the other side. Bear left, signed 'Jumbles Country Park' back to the car park where the walk started.

Walk 15
WYCOLLER

*T*here is a remarkable amount of variety packed into the three miles of this short walk. It has been the custom to divide areas into three ever since Caesar so partitioned Gaul. This walk sticks with tradition by falling neatly into three parts. The first is across the bleak and austere moorland and the exploration is made worthwhile by the far ranging views over the surrounding towns and countryside to brooding Pendle beyond. The route then drops into a valley or clough and the beckside path descends through attractive woodland. The third part of the walk is the exploration of Wycoller, a village that died and was reborn and is of great historic interest. The return to the start is a short, sharp climb but a good tea in the village will give you the energy to tackle this.

The exceptionally attractive, traditional Tea Rooms are behind the Craft Centre, in Wycoller, housed in an old cottage. The interior is cosy on the chilly, damp days for which the Pennines are renowned and there are some tables outside where you can enjoy any welcome sunshine. Delicious cakes are on display to tempt you. For lunch there is a wide choice including a ploughman's with cheese and pickles or a farrier's lunch with smoked sausages. In this most traditional of places, a welcome suggestion is pie and peas, served the Lancashire way with pickled red cabbage. Open every day except Monday (open on bank holidays) throughout the year between 10.30 am and 5 pm. Telephone: 01282 868395.

DISTANCE: 3 miles.
MAP: OS Landranger 103 Blackburn and Burnley or Outdoor Leisure 21 South Pennines.
STARTING POINT: Haworth Road car park (GR 936393).
HOW TO GET THERE: At the Emmott Arms on the A6068 Colne–Keithley road at Laneshaw Bridge, 2 miles east of Colne, take a minor road signed 'Wycoller Country Park'. Drive along the lane for 1½ miles to a car park on the right.
ALTERNATIVE STARTING POINT: There is no parking in Wycoller and only residents' cars or those on business in the village are allowed access.

THE WALK

1. With your back to the road, go out of the bottom left hand corner of the car park to pick up a path leading left along the hillside. When the path forks immediately after a tumbledown wall, fork right downhill. Continue round the hillside as a path joins on the right to a ladder stile over a wall and carry on, walking from stile to stile, to a drive.

The rocks above and to the left are called Foster's Leap, but I have not been able to discover who Foster was or why and when he leapt.

2. Turn right. The drive shortly leads to a gate to the right of Foster's Leap Farm. Through the gate bear left and follow a waymarked path towards another farm to find a footbridge over a stream.

3. Cross the footbridge and turn immediately left on a rough track – don't go up to the farm – and walk with the stream on your left to a gate and stile giving onto a cross track.

4. Turn right, signed 'Bridleway to Trawden Pendle Way'. After some 100 yards, bear right on a path signed 'Footpath to Wycoller Pendle Way'. Walk with a wall on your right to a gate. Through the gate continue ahead on a well-defined path. Ignore a path on the

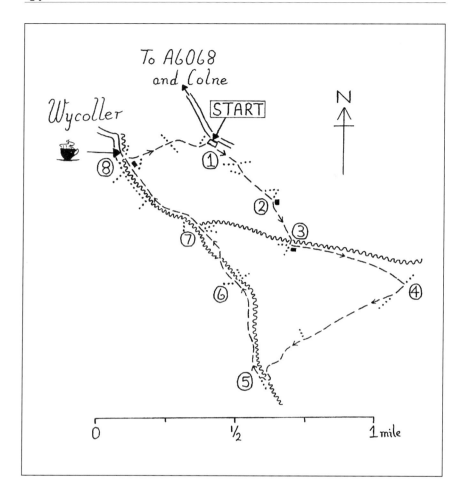

To A6068
and Colne

Wycoller

START

N

8

1

2

3

7

6

4

5

0   ½   1 mile

right signed 'Wycoller' and continue ahead between walls. Descend to cross a stream and climb the other side as far as a gate on the right.

5. Go through the gate. The path bears slightly right, along the top of the clough. A post with arrows on it shortly shows the line and the path itself becomes more clearly defined and enters an attractive wood.

6. When the path reaches a footbridge, do not cross it. Instead, cross

The packhorse bridge at Wycoller.

a stile on the left and continue downstream to a second footbridge. Cross this and press on downstream on the opposite side to join a surfaced track.

7. Turn left into Wycoller, passing the remains of Wycoller Hall. Cross the packhorse bridge and walk through the village to the teashop in a craft centre on the right.

There has been a village here for hundreds of years, as three of its seven bridges illustrate. The oldest is the clam bridge on the left as you approach the village. It is thought to be over 1,000 years old and is protected as an Ancient Monument. In 1989 it was swept away in a flash flood and broken into two. It was repaired only for the same thing to happen again in 1990. It was restored and replaced the following year. Don't be deceived by the rather precarious appearance of the narrow packhorse bridge: it has stood here since the 13th century and has withstood constant use and flash floods for the intervening 700 years. Its appearance is an optical effect of the way the arches are built. The third bridge of historic interest is the clapper bridge of stone slabs supported on stone piers. It dates from the late 18th or early 19th century.

At this time Wycoller was a thriving community of handloom weavers. As the trade became industrialised, the workers were forced to leave to seek employment in the mills. The village became more or less deserted and there was talk of flooding the valley by damming Wycoller Beck. The water authorities bought it for this purpose. The reservoir scheme was fortunately abandoned and the land sold to Lancashire County Council in 1973, who have developed it as a country park. The cottages have been restored and the magnificent aisled barn, the best in the county, is being renovated as an information centre. As all romantic ruins should, Wycoller Hall has a resident ghost. On stormy nights a cavalier horseman is supposed to gallop up to the Hall. Soon afterwards, a woman in black scurries across the clapper bridge, only to leave almost immediately, issuing piercing shrieks as she heads for the moors. More certain is that Charlotte Brontë visited the area and based Ferndean Manor in 'Jane Eyre' on Wycoller Hall so it is now a place of pilgrimage for fans of the Brontë sisters. The 9-mile Brontë Way has been created to link Wycoller and Haworth.

One more recent resident was Tom Emmott, who lived in Wycoller Cottage, next to Wycoller Hall. He lived in a fantasy world: his claims of a degree from London University and service in Military Intelligence were products of his imagination, as was his boast that his economic views had been forwarded by the Chancellor of the Exchequer to the World Monetary Conference. He founded the Lancastrian Party and stood in the 1959 General Election, polling nearly 200 votes. Perhaps this is an indication that there is support for Home Rule for Lancashire!

8. From the teashop turn left and recross the packhorse bridge. Take a path that goes to the left of the derelict Hall. Go up some steps on the left to join a broad, fenced track, originally a carriage route to the Hall. Follow this uphill to a large wooden kissing-gate on the right giving into the car park where the walk started.

It is hard to imagine that this steep and now rather rough track was once the carriage entrance to Wycoller Hall. Note the unusual slab walls, which you may have noticed elsewhere on the walk. They are believed to originate from the 12th century when commercial cattle farms, known as vaccaries, were established in East Lancashire.

Walk 16
FOULRIDGE

*T*his is a very pleasant and easy route with lots of waterside walking – the Leeds and Liverpool Canal and two reservoirs. These are connected by quiet field paths and tracks making a most attractive ramble with the opportunity to inspect an engineering triumph of the canal age and perhaps – if you time your walk right – enjoy a trip on the canal.

 Foulridge Wharf Tearooms incorporate a traditional craft bakery that uses organic produce as much as possible and this is reflected in the quality of the bread and especially the outstanding scones, which are offered in several varieties. There are also cakes and other teatime goodies. For lunch sandwiches are served, with soup if you wish, as well as full meals. The teashop is housed in the former Wharfmaster's Office and the stables for the horses that towed the barges. There are some tables outside at the front, overlooking the canal, and some more at the back, overlooking fields. Open between 10 am and dusk every day except Monday in summer; also open for the same hours in December, reflecting the popularity of the Christmas lunches. For the rest of the winter, between October and Easter, the teashop is open from Thursday to Sunday. Telephone: 01282 869159.

When the teashop is closed, the Hole In The Wall pub, passed en route in Foulridge, serves food.

DISTANCE: 3 miles.

MAP: OS Landranger 103 Blackburn and Burnley or Outdoor Leisure Sheet 41 Forest of Bowland and Ribblesdale.

STARTING POINT: Slipper Hill Reservoir (GR 875417).

HOW TO GET THERE: From the A56 on the northern outskirts of Colne, turn west on Regent Road. Continue over a roundabout and mini-roundabout. Turn right, signed 'Sailing Club ½ Foulridge 1'. Immediately before a house turn left along an even smaller lane for ¼ mile to a pull-off on the left just before a stone bridge over a stream and Slipper Hill Reservoir on the right.

ALTERNATIVE STARTING POINT: If you wish to visit the teashop at the beginning or end of your walk, there is ample free parking at Foulridge Wharf, reached from the A56 north of Colne. You will then start the walk at point 7.

THE WALK

1. Continue along the lane over the bridge. Some 20 yards after the bridge turn right over a stepped slip stile on a path waymarked with a witch symbol. Walk up to the reservoir then turn right beside it. Continue on the path when the reservoir ends, crossing a surfaced drive to a house on the right. The rough path climbs gently.

2. As the track bears left, bear right up a grassy bank to a gated slit stile, again waymarked with the witch symbol. Walk along the right hand side of two fields to a stile onto an entrance drive. Cross to a stile opposite.

3. Over the stile turn left for 25 yards then cross a stile on the right into a field. Head diagonally left to a small gate and steps onto a lane.

4. Turn right for about 80 yards. At a right hand bend at a letter box, continue ahead on a farm track that ends at two gates.

5. Go through the gate on the right onto a fenced track downhill then on across a field and across a bridge over a canal. This is the Leeds and Liverpool Canal (see Walk 11).

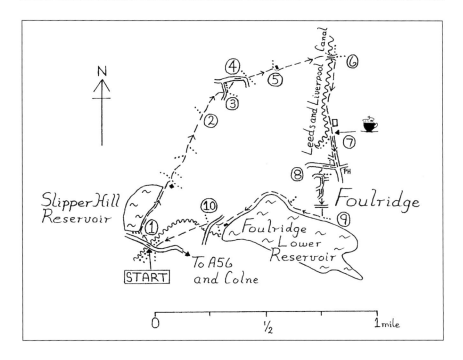

 6. Turn right on the canal towpath to the teashop at Foulridge Wharf.

Foulridge is at the summit of the Leeds and Liverpool Canal. Rather than add to the 91 locks that carry the canal over the Pennines, the engineers decided it would be cheaper to tunnel here. Opened in 1796, Foulridge Tunnel is almost a mile long and its construction was an engineering triumph of the canal age. There is no towpath. Originally the bargees had to propel their boats through by 'walking' on the walls, known as 'legging it', while the horses were led over the hill to rejoin their barge on the other side. A steam tug replaced this arduous task in 1880. In 1912 a cow called Buttercup fell into the canal at the Barrowford end and swam through the tunnel to emerge none the worse at the Foulridge end.

7. Turn left out of the tea shop along a road rather than the tow path. At the Hole In The Wall pub turn right along the B6251, Barnoldswick Road, for 100 yards.
   Note: To see the entrance to Foulridge Tunnel continue along the towpath.

The Leeds and Liverpool Canal at Foulridge.

8. Turn left along a track signed as a Private Road and called Waller Hill, through to a road. Turn left, follow the road round to the right then keep going in the same direction, ignoring all side turns. When the road ends, press on along a path, crossing another road to a reservoir.

9. Turn right round the reservoir as far as the Sailing Club House.

When a canal is in use it constantly loses water and therefore has to be topped up. For this reason there are always compensation reservoirs associated with canals. The two reservoirs on the route were built for this purpose. Select houses have been built overlooking this reservoir, which we are supposed to call Lake Burwain. I suppose this sounds more attractive than Foulridge Compensation Reservoir!

10. Walk down through the Sailing Club car park to a lane. Turn left for 25 yards then **fork** right on an unsurfaced track (do not **turn** right on a surfaced track). Follow this to a lane and turn right for a few yards to the start.

Walk 17
BARLEY

This corner of Lancashire is steeped in stories of witches. In the 17th century the whole country was gripped by witch fever. One of the most infamous episodes features a group from Barley and the surrounding district who were hanged in 1612. This walk explores some of the country where these events took place. It is an extremely varied route linking three Pendle villages with woodland and field paths and a walk by a reservoir beneath the brooding bulk of Pendle Hill. The return after tea in Barley is an outstanding river bank walk by Pendle Water.

 Barley Tea Room is a traditional establishment in an 18th century building, complete with exposed beams, where you can be sure of a friendly welcome and good value for money. The scones with cream and jam are substantial and the cakes are tempting. For a light (?) lunch there are sandwiches, served with a generous portion of chips and salad, filled jacket potatoes or broth and dumplings. If you feel the need of something even more filling there are full meals such as Barley brunch, Dales pork sausages with onions or cheese and onion pie. Barley Tea Room is open all year round every day except Monday. It is always open between 11 am and 3 pm and until much later in the lighter summer months. Telephone: 01282 694127.

DISTANCE: 4 miles.

MAP: OS Landranger 103 Blackburn and Burnley or Outdoor Leisure Sheet 41 Forest of Bowland and Ribblesdale.

STARTING POINT: Roughlee school (GR 838399).

HOW TO GET THERE: From the A682 Nelson–Gisburn road at Barrowford take a minor road signed 'Roughlee 1½' to Roughlee. Turn left at a T junction, signed 'Barley 1½' and continue through the village for ½ mile to a parking place on the left, just before some white railings start.

ALTERNATIVE STARTING POINT: If you wish to visit the teashop at the beginning or end of your walk, start in Barley car park. To find the teashop take a path by the public conveniences to the village. The teashop is on the main street on the right. You will then start the walk at point 9 (teashop) or point 10 (car park).

THE WALK

Note: The outward leg involves some steady though undemanding climbing and some stretches can be ferociously muddy, so go prepared.

1. With your back to the river, go left along the lane. Immediately after crossing a bridge over the river, turn right on a path along the river bank and follow it as far as a farm bridge over the river.

2. Turn left on a surfaced drive between farm buildings to a road. Cross the road and continue in the same direction on a signed footpath opposite. This soon ascends to a gate. Through the gate the path is not visible on the ground at the time of writing; it lies along the right hand side of three fields to a farm drive. Cross the drive and continue in the same direction along the right hand side of a fourth field. The stiles that allow you to cross the drive are not obvious; the one onto the drive is a few yards left and on the other side it lies behind two stone pillars.

In the early 17th century there were two families of poverty-stricken ne'er-do-wells living in this area, both headed by old women. The head of one family was Anne Whittle, known as Chattox. In 1612 she was about 80, 'a very old withered spent and decreped (sic) creature, her sight almost gone ... Her lips ever chattering and talking; but no man knew what.' The matriarch of the other brood was Elizabeth Southern, Mother Demdike, blind, shifty and shuffling round the neighbourhood cursing all who displeased her.

Not surprisingly, the authorities already knew about these families and suspicions involving witchcraft had been raised. In March, Alizon Device, Mother Demdike's granddaughter, was hauled before the local magistrate, Roger Nowell, and confessed to witchcraft. She implicated both her grandmother and Chattox. They in turn both confessed and hurled accusations at each other – cows killed with a curse and ale turned sour with a look – implicating themselves further. Chattox and her daughter, Ann Redfearn, Demdike and Alizon were arrested and sent to Lancaster for trial.

Arresting four witches was good work from the magistrate, Roger Nowell's, point of view, but perhaps he could do better! He heard of a gathering on Good Friday at Malkin Tower, the home of Demdike and the Devices. Malkin Tower sounds like a stately home but in reality it was a tumbledown hovel and its location is not now known. Stolen mutton was eaten and a plot hatched to blow up Lancaster Castle and free the imprisoned women. Some 20 individuals were rounded up, including James Device, the halfwit brother of Alizon. James began to rant about the familiar that attended his sister and nine-year-old Jenet named the people who had been present at the gathering. Among the new crop of witches was a surprise – Alice Nutter was an educated and wealthy farmer's wife from Roughlee, quite unlike the rest of the gang. She remained stoically silent throughout the trial and allowed herself to be condemned as a witch without making any defence. Roger Nowell, the examining magistrate, was undoubtedly glad to have her before him, as she had just won a boundary dispute with him. It is said that some of her family was glad to have her out of the way because they wished to inherit property. The most likely explanation for her presence in the vicinity of Malkin Tower on that fateful Good Friday is that, as a good Catholic, she was on her way to Mass. To confess what she was doing would have endangered her co-religionists and she would have been tortured to reveal the priest. Instead, she remained silent and was condemned as a witch. Roger Nowell later recovered the disputed land.

3. At a second farm drive turn right over a cattle grid and walk along the drive to a farm.

4. Immediately before the first building on the left, turn left over a stream to two gates. Go through the small wooden gate on the right and walk with a stream on your right. Just after a fence on the right is replaced by a wall in the second field – and the stream appears to disappear into the wall! – cross a step stile in the wall and bear half left up a field to a stile. Cut across the corner of a field to another stile

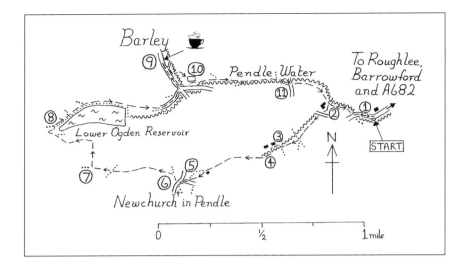

then press ahead with a wood on your right. The path leads behind a house to a stile into a wood. Immediately over the stile go ahead at a fork to a stile out of the wood and on across a field to a stile onto a lane.

5. Turn right, into Newchurch in Pendle.

6. At a road junction turn left for 10 yards then right on a path next to some public conveniences. Watch for a path on the left marked with the witches' symbol of the Pendle Way. Take this. The path is not visible on the ground but strike half right uphill to a stile in the top right hand corner. Over the stile (the highest point of the walk) continue first with a wall and then a fence on the right to a plantation.

This part of the walk is dominated by the brooding presence of Pendle with Barley tucked beneath. At 1,831 feet it just misses being a mountain. Tradition says that if you climb the hill, you must carry a stone to add to the hundreds on top - or be cursed! In 1652 a young man called George Fox made the ascent. At the top he had a vision of Christ gathering people in victory over Satan. From this grew the Society of Friends, more commonly known as the Quakers. He went to Lancaster where, in 1664, he was thrown into the same gaol as the Pendle witches half a century before. His crime was a refusal to take the oath in court on the basis of the words of Jesus,

'Swear not at all'. Only the state religion was permitted so most of the early Quakers spent time in gaol for attending forbidden religious meetings and refusing to pay the church tithes or take the oath in court. Both the Quakers and the witches were seen as a threat to the established order.

7. Turn right over a stile just before the plantation and walk with it on your left to a stile on the left. Go over this into the plantation and follow the well-constructed path to a footbridge at the end of a reservoir. Go over this and ahead to a bridge over a sluice channel to a surfaced track.

8. Turn left and follow the track beside the reservoir and on into Barley. At a road junction turn right to the tea shop on the right.

By modern standards the trial of the witches at Lancaster in August 1612 was a farce. The defendants were mainly uneducated beggars. They had no legal representation. Two, Jane and John Bulcock, were apparently found not guilty by the jury but were nonetheless condemned to hang. The sentence was carried out the next day before an excited crowd. Old Demdike escaped the noose: she died in her cell before the trial opened.

9. Turn left out of the teashop and retrace your steps through the village. At the Pendle Inn take a path on the left parallel with the road and follow it over a river to the large village car park.

10. Go to the entrance to the car park. Take a path signed 'Roughlee' along the right hand side of the car park to a track. Turn left along the track.

11. Immediately after crossing the river at an attractive bridge, turn left to continue by the river, now on the opposite bank, to rejoin the outward route back to the start.

Walk 18
WHALLEY

A quintessential Lancashire walk, this exemplifies all that is best about walking in the Red Rose county. The route wends its way round to Whalley Nab from where there are wide-ranging views of the rural Ribble Valley with Whalley at its base. As well as an outstanding traditional teashop, there are the ancient abbey ruins and the even more ancient church to explore. This is a walk that deserves time to enjoy, to store up memories that will live long after you have completed its 4¹/₂ miles.

The Toby Jug on King Street in Whalley is housed in what may be one of the oldest buildings in the town. It was originally a farm and was probably thatched in those days. After serving many roles it is now an exceptionally charming and well-appointed traditional teashop. The cakes are delicious. There is a variety of set teas including a traditional English tea with tomato or cucumber sandwiches and cake. For lunch there are traditional or open sandwiches or filled ciabatta rolls. The Miller's lunch includes Lancashire cheese with apple and chutney, the Poacher's lunch has pâté and coleslaw while the Angler's lunch features smoked trout. Lunch is served between 11.30 am and 2 pm and The Toby Jug is open from 10 am until 4.30 pm Tuesday to Friday and from 10.30 am until 5 pm on Saturday. Closed Sunday and Monday. Telephone: 01254 823298.

DISTANCE: 4½ miles.

MAP: OS Landranger 103 Blackburn and Burnley or Explorer 19 West Pennine Moors.

STARTING POINT: Spring Wood Picnic Site car park (GR 741360).

HOW TO GET THERE: The car park where this walk starts is on the A671, the Burnley–Whalley road, just under a mile south of its junction with the A59.

ALTERNATIVE STARTING POINT: If you wish to visit the teashop at the beginning or end of your walk, start in Whalley where there is some street parking possible. The teashop is at the south end of the village, just before the bridge over the river. You will then start the walk at point 10.

THE WALK

1. Return to the road and turn left on a path beside the A671. After 200 yards bear left on a minor road, signed 'Sabden'.

2. At a junction, signed 'Burnley 7 Accrington 4¾' to the right, go over a stile to the right of the signpost into a field. At the time of writing the path is not visible on the ground. Bear slightly right over a rise to a second stile. Continue to another stile by a gate then ahead uphill to a gate and stile. Over this stile head down to yet another stile, this one giving onto a surfaced drive.

3. Turn left then, at a T junction with a lane, turn right across Sabden Brook.

4. At the end of the bridge turn right through a small metal gate next to a field gate to walk along a track. Press on as the track becomes less distinct, though still visible, to meet a surfaced drive.

5. Turn right and walk down to a main road. Go straight across to carry on in the same direction along a track. Continue ahead when this becomes a surfaced lane to a T junction with a main road.

6. Turn left across Cock Bridge over the river Calder.

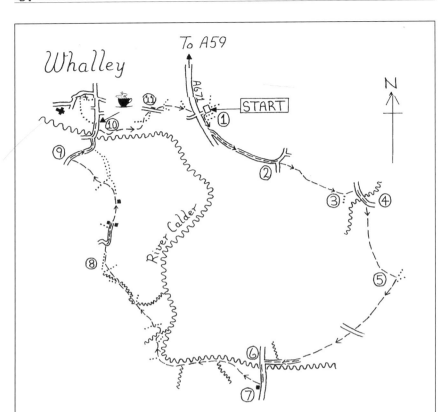

7. Just before the first building on the right, turn right on a path signed 'Whalley Nab'. Bear slightly right on a faint path that leads down to a stile and onto the river bank. Continue by the river – an idyllic spot to linger – all too soon crossing a beck and climbing to a path high above the river. Follow the path above the river until it eventually drops down to a stile and footbridge. Over the footbridge continue ahead with a fence on the right to a line of hawthorns. Turn left in front of these to walk with the trees on the right. Immediately after the last tree turn right. Cross a track leading to gates both left and right and follow the path ahead round the hillside to another

footbridge and on beside a stream to yet another footbridge and stile. Press on beside the stream, now on your right, to two stiles. Go over the one on your right, recrossing the stream to do so. Over the stile bear left uphill to a stile in the top left corner. Don't forget to admire the expanding view behind you as you climb.

8. Over the stile continue on a path to the right of an ancient, sunken track to join a track and then a tiny lane. Keep on in the same direction past some houses where the surface ends. Eventually it becomes a track, follow this round the hillside to a T junction with a lane.

The magnificent viaduct seen ahead carries the Clitheroe–Blackburn line across the river Calder. It is 600 yards long and 70 feet high. It was built in 1850 using 7 million locally produced bricks. It opened with a celebratory run including a coachload of musicians, a Grand Dinner and Ball and a treat for the workforce.

☕ **9.** Turn right to a main road. Turn right over a bridge into Whalley and the teashop on the right.

To visit Whalley church and abbey continue along King Street and turn left along Church Lane.

Whalley is somewhere between a large village and a small town with a history of which a city would be proud. There has been a church here since before the Conquest and it was once at the centre of Lancashire's largest parish. It is a fascinating repository of human interest – well worth a visit. Whalley Abbey is interesting to wander round and a guidebook is available to explain its history and what there is to see. It is open every day from 11 am to 5 pm. Telephone: 01254 822268.

10. Turn left out of the teashop to retrace your steps for 50 yards then turn left along Calder Vale. After the last house bear left to walk upriver. Eventually the path swings away from the river up to a road.

11. Turn right for 50 yards then bear left on a signed path up to a stile. Over the stile bear half left then right at a fork after 20 yards. Follow the increasingly faint path on across a field to a stile that gives onto a strip of woodland and a path to the A671 opposite the car park where the walk started.

Walk 19
WADDINGTON

This walk starts at the edge of Clitheroe, the capital of the Ribble Valley, which is well worth exploring. The route begins beside the river and the first part of this stretch is enlivened by some wooden sculptures. There follows an undemanding climb to a higher level for splendid views across the valley, before dropping down to one of the most beautiful of the villages for tea. The return is an easy stroll on lanes and tracks, passing a building known to Girl Guides worldwide.

The Country Kitchen Café in Waddington is a traditional teashop in the centre of the village. Outside, underneath some amazing hanging baskets, there are a couple of tables from which you can watch the world go by in this popular and attractive spot. A selection of delicious cakes is available, all baked on the premises, and other teatime goodies include teacakes and crumpets as well as that Lancashire favourite, an excellent baked egg custard. There are sandwiches and filled jacket potatoes for lunch as well as full meals for the heartier appetite. These include corned beef hot-pot with red cabbage and an all-day breakfast. The Country Kitchen opens at 10 am and closes at 4.30 pm during the week and 5 pm at weekends. In summer it is open every day, just closing on Monday for the rest of the year. Telephone: 01200 429364.

DISTANCE: 4¹/₂ miles.

MAP: OS Landranger 103 Blackburn and Burnley or Outdoor Leisure 41 Forest of Bowland and Ribblesdale.

STARTING POINT: Brungerley Bridge (GR 738429).

HOW TO GET THERE: From Clitheroe take the B6478 towards Waddington to a layby on the right just beyond Brungerley Bridge over the river Ribble.

ALTERNATIVE STARTING POINT: If you wish to visit the teashop at the beginning or end of your walk, start in Waddington where there is limited street parking. The teashop is on the main street almost opposite Coronation Garden. You will then start the walk at point 9.

THE WALK

Until the beginning of the 19th century, there was no bridge here and travellers had to use stepping stones, known as the Hipping Stones. To ensure a water supply for the cotton mills of Clitheroe, a dam was built downstream at Eddisford. This raised the level of the river and the stones were submerged so a bridge was built in 1801. The present structure was erected in 1816, though it has been widened and altered many times since.

1. Return to and cross the bridge. Continue along the road as far as the end of the first field on the left then turn left on a surfaced track through ornamental metal gates, signed 'Ribble Way'. Follow the path, bearing left at a fork, to follow the river bank as far as the next bridge and a road.

Sculptures can be seen from this path and more will be found if you explore the paths to the right. The Sculpture Trail was launched in 1993 following a seven month residence by artist Thompson Dagnall. Since then other artists and local people have contributed more pieces. This part of the river was very popular in the past. Rowing boats could be hired and there were bathing huts! Dagnall's main piece is 'Saving Sheep' on the bank of the river. It portrays a shepherd rescuing a sheep from the river and it is on the site of the bathing huts.

2. Turn left over the bridge and walk along the road into West Bradford.

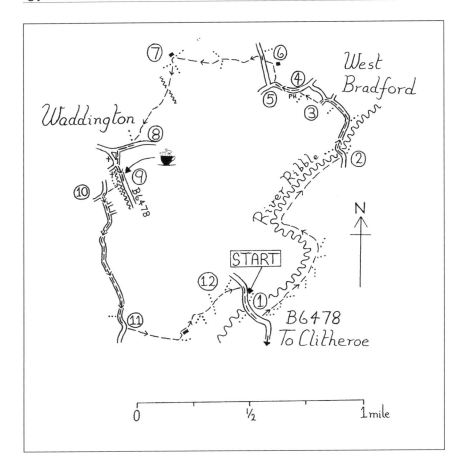

3. Turn left along Mill Street. At the end turn right on a path and follow it through to a road.

4. Turn left.

5. As the road bends left, turn right along a track. Follow it round to the left to a lane.

6. Turn right for 60 yards then turn left on a signed path starting up steps. Go along the right hand side of the first field and continue by a fence in a second. When the fence ends continue ahead to a stile.

Over the stile, skirt right to a three-way path junction in the far right corner of the field. Take the middle one to in effect continue in the same direction along the left hand side of a field to a stile. Over this stile bear half right towards a farm to a gate onto a farm track in front of the farmhouse.

7. Turn left. At a junction with a track on the right, go over a stile to the left of a field gate. Head diagonally down a field to a footbridge over a stream then press on in the same direction to pick up a fence on the left. Walk beside it to a gate and on to a gate into a farmyard. Bear right to a road.

8. Turn right. Fork left then continue down through Waddington to the teashop on the left.

On the right as you enter the village is Waddington Hospital. These trim cottages round three sides of an open green were built at the beginning of the 18th century for the widows of employees of the local gentry, the Parkers. The scope has been widened since, of course, but they are still available to retired and single women. The original Foundation laid down that the widows should attend daily worship and a beautiful chapel was provided for this.

9. Turn left out of the teashop and continue along the road. Go into the Coronation Garden on the right at the War Memorial and cross a bridge over the stream that runs through the centre of the village. Turn left. Go through a small gate out of the gardens and immediately turn right up some steps. Go through a gate at the top and across a field to a gate onto a road.

A stream and the beautifully maintained public gardens, which commemorate the accession to the throne of Queen Elizabeth II, enhance the main street. Across the road is Waddington Hall, which played a dramatic role in English history. Henry VI was an incompetent monarch, especially for the turbulent times at the end of the 15th century when the Lancastrian and Yorkist factions were vying for power. His personality was better suited to be a monk or scholar and he was prone to fits of insanity. Following his defeat at the Battle of Hexham in 1464 he fled to his supporters and ended up staying at Waddington Hall under the protection of the Tempest family. He was warned that the Yorkist supporters of Edward IV were coming for him and had to flee, apparently leaving his dinner on the table.

Waddington.

10. Turn left, then left again after 50 yards, signed 'Clitheroe 1½ Mitton 4'. Walk out of the village along the road for ½ mile, ignoring roads on the left.

11. Turn left through a gate on a signed path along a track (at the time of writing the sign has fallen from its post and is propped up on the wall). At Waddow Hall, now owned by the Girl Guide Association, the path leaves the track to the left to go behind the buildings and then rejoins it. Continue along what is now a surfaced drive, ignoring surfaced tracks to left and right.

12. Do not go as far as the road but bear right on a surfaced track that leads to a stile onto the road. Turn right, back to the start.

Henry VI got as far as the Hipping Stones before Sir Thomas Talbot and his son captured him. Their reward was £100 and a pension of £40 a year. The King was strapped to his horse and taken to the Tower of London, where he was held for five years. The Earl of Warwick restored him to the throne as a puppet in 1470: in the words of one chronicler, 'the King was as mute as a crowned calf'. He was defeated again at the Battle of Barnet in 1471 and returned to the Tower where he was executed.

Walk 20
NEWTON AND SLAIDBURN

*T*o call this part of the Hodder Valley one of the loveliest parts of *Lancashire would deeply offend many traditionalists, although none would deny the beauty of the landscape or the charm of Slaidburn and Newton. The reason they would dispute my description is that it was severed from Yorkshire by administrative fiat and given to Lancashire. I, for one, am happy to own it, if for no other reason than to include this excellent walk in this book! The two villages referred to do not lie on the direct route but both are attractive and worth a few steps diversion to explore.*

The Riverbank Tearooms, on the edge of Slaidburn, is a deservedly popular refreshment stop with walkers, cyclists and visitors to this attractive riverside location. It is ideally situated overlooking the village green and river Hodder. There is seating upstairs but many choose to enjoy their tea and cakes outside. A good selection of delicious cakes is available, including an outstanding banana toffee pie, which may be supplemented by sandwiches or the ever popular bacon butties. Full meals are also served, among them the Lancashire favourite of cheese and onion pie. Open between 10.30 am and 5 pm throughout the year. Telephone: 01200 446398.

DISTANCE: 4½ miles.

MAP: OS Landranger 103 Blackburn and Burnley or Outdoor Leisure 41 Forest of Bowland and Ribblesdale.

STARTING POINT: Bridge over the river Hodder at the south end of Newton. There is limited parking by the bridge on the side away from the village (GR 698502). There is also very limited street parking in Newton.

   If these prove impossible, start in Slaidburn, where there is a large public car park, and visit the tea shop at the start or finish of the walk.

HOW TO GET THERE: Newton and Slaidburn are both on the B6478, the Clitheroe–Long Preston road.

ALTERNATIVE STARTING POINT: If you wish to visit the teashop at the beginning or end of your walk, start in Slaidburn, where there is ample parking in a public car park at the east end of the village. The teashop is next to the car park. You will then start the walk at point 10.

THE WALK

1. With your back to the bridge and the village, take an unsigned path next to a field gate on the left to walk upstream. Continue on the path as the river veers away as far as a gate into a field. Walk along the left hand side of the field to a footbridge over a tributary of the Hodder to pick up a track.

2. When the track forks, take neither branch but go over a stile in the fork into a field. Head across to the right of farm buildings seen ahead to find a gate onto a lane.

3. Turn left.

4. Immediately after a large stone barn, take a path on the right leading through the farmyard of Manor House Farm. Walk along a track from the farm, bearing left as a track joins from the right, as far as a bridge across a river – Easington Brook.

5. Do not cross the river but turn left to follow a path along the left bank of the river until it ends at a stile into a field.

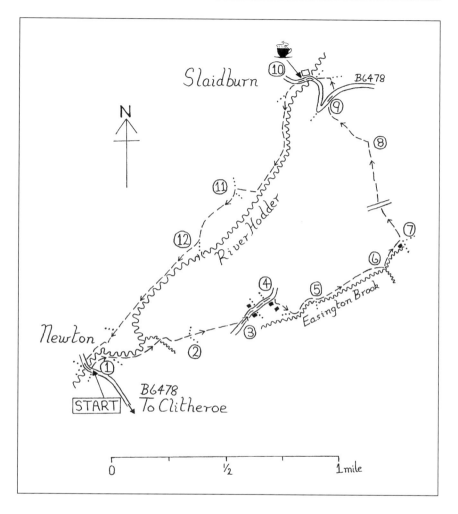

6. Cross the stile and walk along the right-hand side of the field to a gate into a farmyard and through it to a surfaced drive.

7. Turn left to a lane. Cross the lane and press on in the same direction, climbing up the left-hand side of a field. There are constantly expanding views of the lovely Hodder Valley, with Newton beyond the wooded crag of Great Dunmow, which the route passes on the return leg. At the top, go through a gate on the left to continue in the same direction, now with a wall on the right, to a stone stile beside a field gate.

8. Over the stile turn left. When Slaidburn comes into view below, bear to the right of a large depression and down the field to a gate onto a road.

9. Turn right for 70 yards then cross a stile on the left to follow a signed path down a field and back to the road. Turn right over a bridge to Slaidburn and the teashop on the right.

It is well worth taking time to stroll round Slaidburn. With a population of about 500, it is the largest community on the Hodder. The pub used to be called The Dog. A 19th century Master of the Hunt heard a hound calling and remarked "Hark to Bounty" and the name stuck. As well as its unusual name, the pub has another unique feature. A room upstairs was the courtroom of the Forest of Bowland where poachers were tried and which is said to have been used by Cromwell. It was used as recently as 1937 to try petty crimes and is still intact. The church is mainly 15th century, replacing an earlier Norman building on the same site. Of special interest is the Angel Stone. Carved with a figure and swastika, it is a monument to the memory of the Norsemen who invaded north-west England in AD 950.

10. Turn right out of the teashop. When the road bends sharp right, turn left on a signed path next to the Wesleyan chapel. The public footpath soon bears right away from the river but there is a permissive path along the bank. Follow this until it leads away from the river at a waterworks to meet a track.

11. Turn left along the track, ignoring a signed river bank path after 30 yards.

12. As the track approaches a bridge, turn right off the track to walk along the bottom of a steep slope. This path ultimately leads to the river. Do not follow the river bank for long – the river makes a large meander here. Instead, keep close to a wall on the right and follow the path back to the river and ahead to the bridge where the walk started.